Too Late for Logic

Too Late for Logic is a sweeping and important play, a marvellous portrait of family life and a cunning mix of fact and fiction. Christopher has sacrificed much to haul himself up the academic ladder. As the play opens, he has been asked to deliver a key lecture on Schopenhauer, but Cornelia is dead and Michael has disappeared on a drinking bout with his father's pistol in his pocket. With his career at make-or-break point, Christopher's family is not helping. A marvellously inventive play full of compassion and humour.

Too Late for Logic premiered at the Abbey Theatre, Dublin, in October 1989. This revised edition was first performed at the King's Theatre, Edinburgh, in August 2001.

'A major new play . . . these scenes are beautifully imagined, ache with feeling, and flower into incidents of piercing sadness or absurd laughter' *The Times*

'*Too late for Logic* becomes a life-wish in which words are, quite literally, disarming' *Observer*

'One of his most disturbing, affecting and subjective plays' *Irish Times*

Tom Murphy's work includes a *A Whistle in the Dark*, *Famine*, *The Morning After Optimism*, *The Sanctuary Lamp*, *Conversations on a Homecoming*, *The Gigli Concert*, *Bailegangaire*, *Too Late for Logic*, *She Stoops to Folly* and *The Wake*. His career has been markedly associated with the Irish National Theatre (the Abbey Theatre). He was born in Tuam, Co. Galway. He lives in Dublin.

Published by Methuen 2001

1 3 5 7 9 10 8 6 4 2

First published in 1990 by Methuen Drama

This edition, with revisions, published in 2001 by
Methuen Publishing Limited,
215 Vauxhall Bridge Road, London SW1V 1EJ

Copyright © 1990, 2001 Tom Murphy

The author has asserted his moral rights.

Methuen Publishing Limited Reg. No. 3543167

A CIP catalogue record for this book is available from the British Library

ISBN 0 413 63220 2

Typeset by SX Composing DTP, Rayleigh, Essex
Printed and bound in Great Britain by Cox and Wyman Ltd, Berkshire

Caution

Tom Murphy

Too Late for Logic

Methuen Drama

Edinburgh International Festival

The Edinburgh International Festival was founded in 1947 in the aftermath of a devastating world war. The founders believed that the Festival should enliven and enrich the cultural life of Europe, Britain and Scotland and provide a platform for the flowering of the human spirit.

The programmes of the Festival were intended to be of the highest possible standard presented by the best artists in the world. The achievement of those aims over the years has ensured the Edinburgh International Festival is now one of the most important cultural celebrations in the world.

Now, in this new millennium both the political world and the world of the arts are very different from the immediate post war years, and the Festival has developed significantly in the interim. However, the founders' original intentions are closely reflected in the current aims and objectives of the Festival which continues to bring huge economic, cultural and social benefits to the City of Edinburgh and Scotland as a whole.

Royal Lyceum Theatre Company

The Royal Lyceum Theatre Company was formed in 1965 with the first production *The Servant o' Twa Maisters* opening on 1 October. The Company was the first to receive civic support and has been a major force in Scottish and British drama for over thirty years, providing Edinburgh with the highest standard productions from a wide classical and contemporary repertoire. The Royal Lyceum Theatre Company is involved with the most talented of Scotland's actors, directors and designers and helps train Scotland's best young theatre practitioners.

The Edinburgh International Festival gratefully acknowledges support from:

Grants

Principal Supporters

Dunard Fund
Edinburgh International Festival Endowment Fund

Sponsors

Bank of Scotland
BT Scotland
Caledonian Brewery
Corporate Communication Hire Ltd
IBM
The List
Lloyds TSB Scotland
NEC
Renault U.K.
The Royal Bank of Scotland
Scottish & Newcastle plc
Scottish Life
ScottishPower
Scottish Widows
Standard Life
Tayburn

Proscenium Club Members

Baillie Gifford
The Balmoral Hotel
Bank of Scotland
Caledonian Hilton
Dunfermline Building Society
Edinburgh Airport Limited
Edinburgh Chamber of Commerce
Edinburgh Fund Managers
Ethicon Limited
Gerrard Limited
INTELLIGENT FINANCE
MacDonald Orr Limited
Maclay Murray & Spens
Martin Currie Investment
Management Limited
Meconic plc
John Menzies plc
The Miller Group Ltd
Morrison Group Ltd
Norwich Union Insurance
Pillans & Wilson
Scottish & Newcastle plc
ScottishPower
Scottish Provident
Scott-Moncrieff
Sheraton Grand Hotel
Standard Life
Turcan Connell WS
Walter Scott & Partners

Principal Donors

American Friends of the Edinburgh
International Festival
Edinburgh International Festival
Capital Fund
Edinburgh Military Tattoo

Trusts and Foundations

l'AFAA
Abbey National Charitable Trust
The Binks Trust
The Britten Estate Limited
The John S Cohen Foundation
CoPEC
Cruden Foundation Limited
The Cultural Office of the Spanish
Embassy UK
The Peter Diamand Trust
The Evelyn Drysdale Charitable Trust
Goethe Institut
The Hamada Edinburgh Festival
Foundation
Miss K M Harbinson's Charitable Trust
Institut Français d'Ecosse
Eda, Lady Jardine Charitable Trust
Lloyds TSB Foundation for Scotland
Miss Helen Isabella McMorran
Charitable Settlement
Peter Moores Foundation
The Morton Charitable Trust
The Negaunee Foundation
The Oppenheim Foundation
P F Charitable Trust
Risk Charitable Fund
The Russell Trust
Scotland's Year of the Artist
Stanley Thomas Johnson Foundation
The Stevenston Charitable Trust
Miss C A Sym's Charitable Trust
Thirkleby Trust

Donors

Jenners
Johnston Press plc
KPMG
Mactaggart & Mickel
The Miller Group Ltd
NEC

In Kind Supporters

Matthew Algie & Company Ltd
Capital solutions...
Dimensions (Scotland) Ltd
Energizer UK
Glenmorangie
Lever Fabergé
Martin's Restaurant
Nokia UK Ltd
Orange S.A.
Prestonfield House Hotel
Strathmore Mineral Water Co.
Tullis Russell Papermakers

Edinburgh International Festival Muses

Platinum Supporters
Mr and Mrs James Anderson
Mr J S Bevan
The Hon. Lord Clarke
Mr Richard W Colburn
Sir Gerald and Lady Elliot
Mr Andrew Fletcher
Mr and Mrs Ted W Frison
Ian and Dorothy Godden
Mr and Mrs Fred Johnston
Mr Derek H Moss
Sir John and Lady Shaw
Dr Marshall and Mrs Mary Smalley
Iain Somerville
Mr Jim and Mrs Isobel Stretton
Ms Deirdre Whiteside
Mr Hedley G Wright

Lloyds TSB
Scotland

We should like to thank Lloyds TSB Scotland for its ongoing and highly valued support and for making these performances of *Too Late for Logic* possible.

We are delighted that the company has continued to express its belief in and commitment to the importance of the arts in the life of the community in this way.

Many heartfelt thanks for this wonderful support.

Brian McMaster
Festival Director

supporting your role

We wish you every success and are delighted to give you all the behind-the-scenes support you need.

Lloyds TSB
Scotland
Your life. Your bank.

Lloyds TSB Scotland plc, Henry Duncan House, 120 George Street, Edinburgh EH2 4LH.
A member of the Banking Ombudsman Scheme and a signatory to the Banking Code.

Edinburgh International Festival presents the
Royal Lyceum Theatre Company in

Too Late for Logic

By **Tom Murphy**

Christopher	**Duncan Bell**
Michael	**Hugh Ross**
Patricia/Maud	**Jennifer Black**
Monica	**Juliet Cadzow**
Geoffrey/Wally	**Sandy Neilson**
Jack	**Gregory Finnegan**
Petra	**Jo Freer**
Tony	**Matt Costello**
Moreva	**Emma Neilson**
Director	**Patrick Mason**
Designer	**Francis O'Connor**
Lighting Designer	**Paul Keogan**
Fight Arranger	**Richard Ryan**
On book	**Ruth Crighton**

First performed by The Abbey Theatre, Dublin at the
Dublin Theatre Festival on Tuesday 3 October 1989.

First performance of this new production opened at the
King's Theatre, Edinburgh on Monday 13 August 2001.

Performances:
Monday 13 – Saturday 18 August 7.30pm
& Saturday 18 August 2.30pm

Performances sponsored by

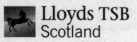

An Edinburgh International Festival Production.

Tom Murphy

Tom Murphy's work includes *A Whistle in the Dark* (1961), *On the Outside* (1962), *A Crucial Week in the Life of a Grocer's Assistant* (1966), *Famine*, *The Orphans* (both 1968), *The Morning After Optimism* (1971), *The White House* (1972), *On the Inside* (1974), *The Sanctuary Lamp* (1975), *The J Arthur Maginnis Story* (1976), *Epitaph Under Ether* (1979), *The Blue Macuschla* (1980), *The Informer* (adaptation, 1981), *Conversations on a Homecoming*, *The Gigli Concert* (both 1983), *The Seduction of Morality* (novel, 1984), *Bailegangaire* (1985), *Too Late for Logic* (1989), *The Patriot Game* (1991), *She Stoops to Folly* (adaptation, 1995), *The Wake* (1998) and *The House* (2000). He was born in Tuam, County Galway, He lives in Dublin and is a member of Aosdána and the Irish Academy of Letters.

Duncan Bell *Christopher*

National Theatre productions include *Remembrance of Things Past* and *All My Sons*. At the Almeida he played Willie Oban in *The Iceman Cometh* and Lazar in *Plenty*. Last year he appeared at the Lyceum in *Phaedra*. He has also worked for The Traverse, Cheek by Jowl, the RSC, The Royal Exchange, The Old Vic, Sheffield Crucible, York Theatre Royal, Bristol Old Vic, and English Touring Theatre. His television credits include *Where The Heart Is*, *Life Support*, *Taggart*, *Soldier Soldier*, *Hornblower*, *Bramwell* and *Between the Lines*.

Jennifer Black *Patricia/Maud*

Trained at the Royal Scottish Academy of Music and Drama. Theatre includes *The Bench*, *House Among the Stars*, *Kill the Old Torture Their Young*, *Family* (Traverse), *Ashes to Ashes* (Ghostown), *The Trick is to Keep Breathing* (Tron, Royal Court, Du Maurier Festival, Toronto), *Good*, *The Baby*, *Lavotchkin 5* (Tron), *Buried Treasure* (Bush), and *Carmen: The Play*, *Sacred Hearts* (Communicado). Previous Royal Lyceum Theatre productions include *Macbeth*, *Peter Pan*, *STIFF!*, *An Experienced Woman Gives Advice*, *Dead Funny*, *On Golden Pond*, *Blithe Spirit*, and *Trivial Pursuits*. TV & Film work include: *Tinseltown, I Saw You*, *The Bill*, *Taggart*, *Hi-De-Hi*, *Local Hero*, and *Heavenly Pursuits* and radio includes *Week-Ending*, various short stories and radio adaptation of *The Trick is to Keep Breathing*. Jennifer Black's directing credits include an award-winning production of *Orphans* at the Edinburgh Festival Fringe and a specially commissioned Stuart Paterson version of Zola's *Thérèse Raquin* (Communicado), which was revived in Autumn 1998 as a co-production with the Royal Lyceum Theatre.

Juliet Cadzow *Monica*

Theatre work includes *The Gigli Concert* by Tom Murphy at Teatro Trianon, Rome, *Border Warfare* (Wildcat at The Tramway, directed by John McGrath), *The Ship* and *The Big Picnic* (Bill Bryden at The Shed), *The Indian Queen* (Citizens Theatre); *Conversations with Angels*, and *Entertaining Mr Purcell* (Covent Garden Festival), *A Passionate Woman* (Perth), seasons in Sicily and Rome with La Zattera di Babele, and productions at the Traverse Theatre, Dundee Rep, and Wildcat. Royal Lyceum Theatre productions include Jean Brodie in *The Prime of Miss Jean Brodie*, Madam Arcati in *Blithe Spirit*, and roles in *An Ideal Husband*, *Tartuffe*, *The Odd Couple*, *As You Like It*, and *Comedy of Errors*. Previous Edinburgh International Festival appearances include *Ane Satyre of the Thrie Estaites*, *Macbeth* on Inchcolm island, and *The Satire of the Four Estates*, by John McGrath. Television appearances include Rosa Rossi in *Glasgow Kiss*, *Always and Everyone*, *The Bill*, *Casualty*, *Rab C Nesbitt*, *Life Support*, *Coronation Street*, *Taggart*, *Dr Finlay* and *Hamish Macbeth* and film work includes a BAFTA nomination for *Thicker Than Water*: *Venus Peter*, *The Big Man*, *Heavenly Pursuits* and *The Wicker Man*.

Matt Costello *Tony*

Trained at the Royal Scottish Academy of Music and Drama. Theatre work includes *Swing Hammer Swing*, and *Men Should Weep* (Citizens Theatre), *Street Scene*, and *Fate* (Scottish Opera, English National Opera), *No Mean City*, *Revolting Peasants* and *Jump the Life to Come* (7:84), *Danton's Death* (Communicado), *My Brother's Keeper*, *Hansel and Gretel* and *Robin Hood*, (Cumbernauld Theatre) *One Flew Over the Cuckoo's Nest* (Raindog), *Brothers of the Brush* (Wiseguise). Royal Lyceum Theatre appearances include *Woyzeck*, *Guys and Dolls*, *A View from the Bridge*, *Cinderella*, *Romeo and Juliet*, *The Hypochondriak*, *Macbeth*, *Of Mice and Men*, *Hobson's Choice*, and *Shadow of a Gunman*. TV & Film work includes *Small Faces*, *Ruffian Hearts*, *Looking After Jo Jo*, *Life Support*, *This Year's Love*, *The Debt Collector*, *Gregory's 2 Girls*, *Takin' Over the Asylum*, *Bad Boys*, *A Mug's Game*, *Taggart*, *City Lights*, *Rab C Nesbitt*, *The Gift*, *The Long Roads*, *Dad on Arrival*, and *Tin Fish*.

Gregory Finnegan *Jack*

Graduated from The Webber Douglas Academy of Dramatic Art this year, where he played Romeo at the Cliveden Shakespeare Festival, David Copperfield, and Ventroux in *Don't Walk Around in the Nude*.

Jo Freer *Petra*

Graduated this year with a First from The Royal Scottish Academy of Music and Drama. Her roles there included Iphigenia, Jenny in *Men Should Weep*, and the narrator in *Animal Farm*. She also appeared in *Heart's Desire* and *Boule De Suif*, directed by Alison Peebles. Other theatre roles include Marina in *Pericles*, and Caliban in *The Tempest*.

Emma Neilson *Moreva*

Emma has been a member of the Lyceum Youth Theatre for several years. She is going to study at the Central School of Speech and Drama this autumn. LYT productions include *A Midsummer Nights Dream, Porcelain Dolls* and *This Here Now* and Royal Lyceum Theatre appearances include *Cinderella, Romeo and Juliet,* and *The Three Sisters.* Emma Neilson has also appeared in *Ylana's 666, La Bayadere, Tigs, Tell Me About It* and *All That's Left.*

Sandy Neilson *Geoffrey/Wally*

At the Royal Lyceum Theatre he was Knox in *The Anatomist* and Andrew in *Clay Bull.* As a member of the Dundee Rep Ensemble he has played Father Paneloux in *The Plague,* Risopolozhensky in *A Family Affair,* Oberon in *A Misummer Night's Dream* and also had roles in *Cabaret, The Winter's Tale* and *The Weavers.* He was Artistic Director of Fifth Estate Theatre Company. On film and television he has been seen in *The Winter Guest, Cardiac Arrest* and *The Debt Collector.*

Hugh Ross *Michael*

Born and educated in Glasgow, at St Andrew's University and trained at RADA, Hugh Ross' theatre work includes repertory at Leeds, York, Colchester, Manchester, Sheffield and Liverpool. Royal National Theatre appearances include *Battle Royal, Lady in the Dark* and *The Invention of Love* and he played Jacques in the Royal Shakespeare Company production of *As You Like It.* Other roles in London include *Death & the Maiden* (Duke of York's), *Democracy* (Bush Theatre), Gloucester in *King Lear* (Royal Court), Mephistopheles in *Dr Faustus* (Greenwich), Judge Brack in *Hedda Gabler* (Playhouse) and Dr Tambourri in *Passion* (Olivier Award nomination, 1997, Queens). He also appeared in Cheek by Jowl productions of *The CID,* and as Malvolio in *Twelfth Night* (Time Out Award). His television work includes *Invasion Earth, Sharpe, Between the Lines, Absolutely Fabulous, An Ungentlemanly Act, The Advocates, Men Only* and *The Cazalets.* Still to be shown: *Inspector Rebus: Dead Souls, Murder Rooms, Shackleton* and *The Mists of Avalon.* Films include: *Patriot Games, Nightbreed,* and *Trainspotting.* Still to be released are *The Four Feathers, The Memory of Water,* and *Charlotte Gray.* Audio work includes *As You Like It, Macbeth* (title role, Arkangel Shakespeare), Malvolio in *Twelfth Night, Julius Caesar* (BBC Shakespeare Collection), *Midsomer Murders* (6 titles, Chivers Audio Books). Hugh Ross has also recorded over 100 radio plays for the BBC, including *Before and After Summer, On Baby Street* and *The Immortals.*

Patrick Mason *Director*

Now a freelance theatre director, Patrick Mason was artistic director of the National Theatre Society (The Abbey and Peacock Theatres, Dublin) from 1993 until 2000. His most recent productions for the Abbey include *Observe the Sons of Ulster Marching Towards the Somme, The Well of the Saints,* and *Philadelphia Here I Come!* He also directed Tom Murphy's previous plays *She Stoops to Folly* and *The Wake* which played at the Edinburgh International Festival in 1999. His production of Brian Friel's *Dancing at Lughnasa* premiered at the Abbey and toured to Britain, Australia and New York where he received a Tony Award in 1992. His opera work includes the *Silver Tassie* for Opera Ireland, and *Il Trittico* for the English National Opera.

Previous Edinburgh International Festival visits with the Abbey Theatre include: *The Well of the Saints, Observe the Sons of Ulster Marching Towards the Somme* and *The Wake*.

His production of Tom MacIntyre's *The Great Hunger* won a Fringe First.

Francis O'Connor *Designer*

Designed *The Wake* for the Abbey Theatre at the 1999 Edinburgh International Festival. Other work for the Abbey includes *The House* by Tom Murphy, *Freedom of the City, The Importance of Being Earnest* and *The Colleen Bawn*. He has recently worked in Canada and Israel on *Honk*. His work at London's Royal National Theatre includes the sets for *Peer Gynt* and *Closer*. In New York he designed the award winning Garry Hynes production of *Beauty Queen of Leenane*. He won the 1998 Best Designer Award for *Tarry Flynn* and *the Leenane Trilogy*.

Paul Keogan *Lighting Designer*

Productions for the Abbey and Peacock Theatres in Dublin include *Tartuffe, Down the Line, Mrs Warren's Profession, The Tempest,* and *Living Quarters*. For Opera Theatre Company Dublin he has designed for *The Beggars Opera* and *The Lighthouse*. He has also worked with Cois Ceim Dance Co in the USA, Loose Canon, the Almeida, Rough Magic and Mandance.

Richard Ryan *Fight Arranger*

'Master-at Arms' at the Royal Academy of Dramatic Art in London. He has worked on recent productions at the Mercury, Colchester, the RSC, The Royal National Theatre and York Theatre Royal.

Royal Lyceum Theatre Company *Too Late for Logic*

Artistic Director — **Kenny Ireland**

Production
Head of Production — **David Butterworth**
Production Assistant — **Sarah-Jane Grimshaw**
Wardrobe Supervisor — **Shirley Robinson**
Deputy Wardrobe Supervisor — **Karen Sorley**
Costume Makers — **Isobel Skea**
Caitlin Blair
Costume Maintenance/Dresser — **Fiona Clark**
Master Carpenter — **Vian Curtis**
Deputy Master Carpenter — **Mike Oliver**
Scenic Artists — **Lisa Kellet**
Monique Jones
Head of Sound — **Jakob de Wit**
Acting Chief Electrician — **Andy Murray**
Storesman/Driver — **John Davidson**

Stage Management
Company Stage Manager — **Jess Richards**
DSM — **Ruth Crighton**
ASMs — **Angela Wayland**
Gemma Swallow

Administration
Administration Director — **Sadie McKinlay**
Accounts Assistant/Payroll — **Magda Buchan**
Administration Assistant — **Rosie Kellagher**

The Royal Lyceum Theatre Company would like to thank
Elaine Parker, Tom McFall, Andrew Watson, Scott Morris, Clifford Simms.
Jill Baird in the donations department at Edinburgh University Library.
Bill Wallace, acting head of Central Library and Information Services and
  Dan McLeod, Head of Security.
Bill Kincaid and Kathy at Ashvale Kincaid for the loan of a wheelchair.
Mark Prosser, general manager at Invacare for the loan of a wheelchair.
United Closers and Plastics.
Persil, Comfort, Persil Finesse courtesy of Lever Brothers
  for providing wardrobe care.
Scottish and Newcastle International Ltd.
Cameron A V Hire (Glasgow).

Too Late for Logic

Characters

Christopher
Petra
Jack
Patricia
Monica
Michael
Geoffrey
Tony
Maud
Wally
Moreva

The roles of **Maud** and **Wally** can be doubled by the actors playing **Patricia** and **Geoffrey**.

Scene One

'J'ai Perdu Mon Eurydice' sung by Maria Callas introduces the play and continues into this scene.

Christopher, *isolated, fifty, looks bedraggled in his overcoat, an unlit cigarette in one hand and, now from his pocket, a gun in the other: a man with a problem.*

The shadows about the place are like figures. They are figures, come to invade his space. He doesn't appear to notice them – nor they him – though they start to circle him, close on him . . . And there is a report from a gun.

The figures now are like a group talking sadly at a graveside. What they are saying makes no sense; gibberish (e.g. **Petra***'s 'Cigarette a like you would Mum': Mum, would you like a cigarette? – etc. with other character lines, spoken backwards, taken from later in the play) . . .*

Christopher, *minus cigarette and gun, has emerged from among them, smiling, denying that he has done anything: he shakes his head, then checks it to see if it's still there . . .*

Christopher   What has happened here? . . . Not at all. I mean, I am I, you are you, whatever we were to each other we are, still. *Nothing* is what's happened here.

The figures are about to leave. Now they are making sense: 'A drink, everybody?' (**Michael**) *'Yeah!'* (**Petra**) *and appreciative sounds from the others.*

Wait a minute – Hold on! . . . I mean, this is pretty desperate stuff. Oho! . . . I am very well thank you. Hold on – hold on! – We can work this one out! All I was doing was – what was I doing? – was trying to write something – a speech for God's sake, that's all! While trying to give up – (*'smoking': he holds up his cigarette hand*). That's all. I'm very well thank you. I'll prove it! Let's go back a few days, backtrack a little, and I bet you I will. OK? OK. O-righty!

He removes his overcoat to become his former self of a few days ago. In his room: his table, table lamp, telephone and answering machine, small tape recorder, some writing materials and a remote control which he uses to kill the music. His speech is more or less continuous from the above.

Yes, he's writing a speech, preparing a lecture and he goes to his desk with confidence. With *confidence!* Never felt better in his life, at the height of his powers – (*He has picked up his recorder to dictate:*) Draft one: Ahmmm . . . Yes. President, fellow acolytes of IASA, ladies and gentlemen, distinguished guests, viewers, and students of course. Schopenhauer: His Phenomenology of Reproduction, and, Did He Hypostasise the *Ding an sich*? (*To himself:*) Good. Now what? Yes. (*Dictates:*) But, before giving my paper, it would be crass of me if I did not pay tribute to . . . (*To himself:*) Crass of me? Crass? Crass! Tck!

'Tck!' in reaction to the phone that has started to ring. He lifts the receiver and replaces it on the cradle, terminating the call.

What was I saying? Crass, crass – remiss! (*Dictates:*) But, before giving my paper, it would be remiss of me if I did not pay tribute to the head of our department here at Trinity, whose place I take today. I refer of course to my distinguished colleague – and *friend* – Dr Wuzzler who cannot be with us. Unfortunately. Indeed, who is extremely ill in hospital. Alas. (*To himself:*) Knocked down by a bus alas-and-indeed – Yep? (*Dictates:*) The election of this venue – venue-university – by IASA for its second international conference is due in no small measure to the efforts of Professor Wuzzler, to his scholarship and to his remarkable – truly, truly remarkable discovery only last year: the previously unknown about two-day visit by the young Schopenhauer to the little scenic town of Cobh in Co. Cork, in 1802. (*To himself:*) Pause for applause. (*Dictates:*) Woozy, if by any chance you are looking in . . . (*Wonders:*) Remote chance? (*Decides on his first:*) If by any chance you're looking in, thoughts with you, get well soon. (*To himself:*) Good, Christopher. Now what? (*Dictates:*) Here, it may be

appropriate to give a rapid summary of the age
Schopenhauer was born into – in consideration of our lay
brethren (*the viewers*). Arthur Schopenhauer, 1788–1860. An
age where things were happening? Yes. French Revolution
– Concept of Human Rights – man's freedom at last? Came
the Terror. Disillusionment. An age begun in hope, an age
of reason: for nothing. *Egalité, liberté, fraternité,* said the
bishops and princes, our royal arse. (*To himself:*) No-no-no-
no-no. Our royal, our royal, our . . . ? Bottoms for the
moment, don't spoil my flow now. (*Dictates:*) Bottoms for the
moment which they replanked up on thrones. A Bourbon –

The doorbell rings. He listens:

A Bourbon? . . . A Bourbon back in France, who had
learned nothing, forgotten nothing.

The doorbell again.

Tck, Jack Daniels himself! (*Listening, hoping it won't ring again.*)
. . . And as for Napoleon –

The doorbell rings –

(*Going off:*) They took Napoleon to distillers and put a cork to
his spirit. Further . . .

He has gone off to answer the door, dictating as he goes.

Jack *and* **Petra** *are at* (*what is meant to be*) **Christopher**'s
front door. **Jack**'s *finger is pressing the doorbell.*

Jack *is eighteen, old top coat, hanging open, as is the fashion. He has
a close bond with* **Christopher**, *though the slow, single nod of the
head that he is given to, doesn't necessarily mean that he agrees. He is
caught in the middle and is probably trying to hold a balance between
his parents.*

Petra *is making a roll-up. Her conflict with* **Christopher** *is
ongoing. She tries to be polite with him – dainty syllable-by-syllable
delivery – but it doesn't come out right. And she resents*
Christopher's *giving so much attention to* **Jack** *to her exclusion.*
(*Also, there is the usual sibling rivalry between her and* **Jack**.) *Her*

dress is colourful, rag-trade stuff, as is the fashion. She is capable of great tenderness and great rage: a child-woman. She is sixteen.

Petra   He's in there. (*She's containing her anger.*)

Jack   How d'you know that?

Petra   He's in there!

Jack   How d'you know that?!

Petra   Why's your hand still on the fucking bell then?! (*And to herself:*) Geeeesss!

Christopher (*arriving, dictating*)   I thank the devil said Goethe I'm no longer a nipper in so thoroughly a dicked-up world.

Jack (*shyly*)   Hi!

Christopher (*greeting them with up-held hand*)   The masses turned back to religion: feed the birds, tuppence a bag.

Jack   Can we come in a minute?

Christopher (*beckoning them to follow him off, returning to his room*)   Man had lost himself again. (*Off:*) Hard to visualise it so unlike our own times. (*Entering:*) So it became a time of demoralisation and debilitating reverie. (*To* **Jack**, *for* **Jack**'s *admiration of his words:*) Hmm?

Jack   What's? (*Meaning 'what are you preparing?'*)

Christopher   Speech – I – Shh! Hence, hence . . .

Petra   Are we dis-turbing you?

Christopher   Hence the melancholy of the writers, the – oh – the Pushkins! Byrons, Lermontovs. The melancholy of the composers: Schubert, Schumann, Chopin. (*To* **Petra**:) Hmm?

Petra   Mozark?

Christopher   Mozart?

Petra   Mozark!

Christopher (*a little triumph*)   Ah! (*Dictates:*) While Mozart was dancing in the depression of his day as a Shirley Temple in hers. (*He puts the recorder aside.*) Nice, the common touch, humour – But we'll put it away.

Jack   Your rooms are nice.

Christopher (*to* **Jack**)   A speech, it's going to be televised.

Jack   Yeh?!

Christopher   But – my progeny! – tea, a coffee? Long time – Hi!

Jack   Hi!

Christopher (*to* **Petra**)   Hello?

Petra *replies with a bow of her head.*

Christopher   The character or will says Schopenhauer comes from the father, the intellect from the mother.

Petra   Where's Chokki?

Christopher (*vaguely*)   Hmm?

Petra   The dog.

Christopher   Oh, fine, I had to have her put down. (*To* **Jack**:) Big, big opportunity. I'm not going to do the usual dry old academic stuff on it: that's not me at all: it never was. I'm going for the reality principle, all-embracing life, *raw* life and what it means, not hide from it or bury it. I have missed our conversations, Jack. Are you reconsidering returning to university?

An apologetic 'no' from **Jack**.

Petra (*to* **Jack**)   Give us a light. (*For her rollie.*)

Jack   D'you mind if we smoke?

Christopher (*doesn't mind, and absently accepts a cigarette from* **Jack**'s *packet*)   You know, to find the harmonies of words that will present the contradictions in man, and . . . (*Only now wondering why have they called.*) But, tea, coffee? I mean, surprise visit.

Jack *looks at* **Petra**. **Petra**, *smoking, now affects her superiority, waiting to see how the men will deal with the next.*

Jack   Cornelia died at lunchtime, Uncle Michael is going to commit suicide, Mum said would you take care of it.

Christopher   . . . Say that again.

Petra   Cornelia died at lunchtime, *yesterday*.

Jack (*taking her correction*)   Yesterday.

Petra   *In* hos-pit-al.

Christopher   I know she was in hospital.

Petra   Your brother's wife, Mum's sister, she's dead.

Christopher   I'm not disputing the matter.

Jack   Uncle Michael is going to – (*Nods/gestures, meaning commit suicide*). Mum's been trying to phone you.

Petra   To kill himself: do-you-under-stand?

Christopher   The always open door.

Jack   What?

Christopher   Epictetus. Phone him.

Jack   He isn't answering either.

Christopher   Call to his house.

Jack   We called.

Petra   Sev-er-al times.

Jack   He's disappeared . . . Dad?

Christopher (*to himself, meaning he is not getting involved*)   No. (*Then pacing, waving his arms.*) Maybe he's dead already, I don't care!

Jack   No!

Christopher   What?

Jack   He said Saturday.

Christopher   Today is . . . He said what?

Jack   Mum got the news and, because he isn't answering, we drove over. He put on his coat – we thought he was coming with us to the hospital. No. He nodded, did that (*'put a finger like a gun to his head'*) – said 'Saturday, D-Day' and – Phith!

Christopher   Left. (*And nods to himself 'yes, that would be Michael'.*)

Petra   We have been looking for him since.

Christopher   What are the arrangements?

Jack   That's it!

Christopher   What's it?

Jack   Mum can't make them without him. (**Christopher** *doesn't understand.*) He's the husband.

Christopher (*'Oh yes.' Then*)   Saturday, why Saturday?

Jack   He didn't give us time to – (*'ask'*). Phith! It's a good question though.

Petra   Try your philosophy on it.

Jack   D'you think he will?

Petra   Grandad did it.

Christopher (*sharply*)   He was shell-shocked. (*Blows a heavy sigh.*) Michael!

Jack   Didn't he swim too far out to sea one time?

Christopher   And I was the one who nearly got drowned.

Petra   Can you help us?

Christopher   And what about me?

Petra   Do you have any idea where he might be then?

Christopher (*has an idea, but*)   No. (*He's pacing, cigarette in and out of his mouth, his hands in a flap for a light.*) I'm not getting involved.

Petra   Oh, that's great! –

Christopher   Immaterial to me! –

Petra   That's smashing! –

Christopher   I left all this kind of thing behind me six months ago! –

Petra (*to* **Jack**)   Do you hear?!

Christopher   Just when things are beginning to fall into place –

Jack   Wrong end –

Petra   (*You*) Left 'all this kind of thing' behind you: US!

Christopher   Just when I'm finding some *meaning*, some answers –

Petra   You're his brother –

Jack   Wrong –

Petra   His bloodywell, bloodywell, bloodywell brother!

Christopher   No.

Petra   . . . For Mum's sake then?

Christopher   And just when this crucial piece of work –

Petra   For Mum's sake then? –

Christopher   Comes along, that I must prepare –

Petra   At her wits' bloody end –

Christopher   That will most likely be the making of me –

Petra   Run off her bloodywell bloodywell feet! Do you ever pick up that phone or listen to messages on that machine?

Christopher *shakes his head, 'No', he's not getting involved, and turns to* **Jack** *for a light.*

Jack   Wrong end.

Christopher   Oh. No thanks, I gave them up. (*Absently, he keeps the cigarette.*)

Jack   Did you? (*Impressed.*)

Christopher   And drink.

Jack   When?

Christopher   Two days ago.

Jack   New life.

Petra (*to herself*)   Geeesssstupid!

Christopher   Yes, new life! Look! (*Looks at his rooms.*) *This* is where I belong. *My* place. I've had twenty *terrifying* years as caretaker of your troubles. Frightening, fossilising years of domesticity. No more. I count too, *somewhere*, in all this. So: young philosopher – all right, middle-aged – but he's brilliant – I say so! The absurdity and hypocrisy of modesty. Middle-aged philosopher now working purposefully and alone. He has things to say because he has suffered. He's no longer a victim because he's coming up with the answers. The moment he's been waiting for arrives. Head of the department – (*that*) old Wuzzler – is knocked over by a bus. He has to step into the breach at short notice and make a singularly meaningful speech. Will he write that speech *and* deliver it *and* on television? Yes, he will – even if it kills him. At last he's recognised as somebody-who-counts, as somebody-who-matters in this world. Enough to be going on? So no Michael thank you, or those other complicated thorns of kindred in my side. (*He gets his tape recorder and* *dictates*:) Enter Schopenhauer to take to his rooms and have a think about it all.

Petra (*to* **Jack**)   Let's go.

Christopher (*to them*)   Find Michael: d'you think it would be as simple as that?

Petra   Are you coming, Jack?

Christopher (*to* **Petra**)   The *friends* he picks up!

Petra   Kind of you to ask how Mum is. (*She leaves.*)

Christopher (*dictating*)   Ahmmm . . . He sees the world as strife, a never-ending mess. He . . . (*To* **Jack**:) How is your mother?

Jack (*holds a shrug, then completes it with a solemn nod. And:*) Not great.

Christopher   . . . Is his car there?

Jack (*'Oh!'*)   We forgot to check the garage. (*He's about to leave.*) Will we – keep you informed?

Christopher *holds a shrug, then completes it with a nod, 'Yes'.* **Jack** *leaves.* (*Joins* **Petra** *who is outside and they go off on their mission.*)

Christopher   O-righty! (*He doesn't sound so o-righty. Dictates:*) He sits down, yes he sits down to write his masterpiece, *The World as Will and Idea*, which he begins – which he begins modestly enough! – 'The world is my idea.'

The phone is ringing again. He looks at it for a moment, then lifts it fearfully, then replaces it gently.

The world is my idea – (*Dictates:*) by which he does not mean of course that life is a dream, though we can safely say – I think! – that it is akin to dreams. The terms Will and Idea: Let us take Idea first . . .

The lights have been changing during the above – and continue to change – for a passage of time, while **Christopher**, *now in* *dumbshow, continues dictating and making notes . . . He has become engrossed in himself to such degree that he is unaware that the phone has rung again; indeed, the caller,* **Patricia**, *is speaking before he registers it (and it is too late to terminate the message).*

Patricia *materialises gradually. She is a woman so exhausted and unhappy that she is unaware of her own confusion – has she phoned* **Christopher** *or* **Michael**? *– or that she is at times talking to herself.*

Patricia   Christopher . . . Christopher? . . . Michael? . . . (*Smiles.*) Which of you have I dialled? . . . Christopher, this is Patricia again. I'm sorry to bother you, but we still can't find Michael. I've phoned and phoned. I don't know what to do. Doesn't he want to see her? Before they, before they. Doesn't he want to say goodbye . . . I've left messages on his machine, bloody machine . . . your bloody machine. I've left messages everywhere . . . Bloodywell machines . . . I thought love was stronger than death. Doesn't he want to kiss her? . . . (*Smiles.*) Isn't there anybody there? . . . Come away my love my dove my fair one come away with me . . . My beloved is mine and I am his. I thought love was stronger than separation . . . I do not understand . . . Michael? Christopher? . . . Michael, this is Patricia again. I've told them at the hospital that you are abroad, but that I've contacted you and that you are returning. But they are getting very cross: I know it. I've written the ad, the death notice to put in the papers. Does it suit? I don't know. That the remains will be taken to St Helen's at five p.m. That's tomorrow. That the burial will be on Friday at eleven. Does that suit? I hope that suits . . . My love my dove my fair one come away with me . . . I'm taking it in by hand or else it won't appear. To the newspaper office. And to see the undertakers again. *Caskets*, they keep calling them *caskets* . . . I don't know . . . And do you want a limousine? And there are papers to be signed. Always bloody papers. Certificates, affidavits, bloody papers, when someone dies, walks out. Dies . . . I thought that if matters could not be altogether lovely ever again between us, they could at least be pleasant.

At least that . . . *Michael*: There are matters I am not allowed
to discharge on your behalf. I have enough bloodywell
matters of my own in any case. Cornelia was my sister but
she was your wife. For twenty years. Does that not matter –
does that not mean something? Does anything matter? . . .
I'm sorry. (*And a sob escapes. Then:*) But I thought I was
getting over another kind of grief. I thought that winter was
past, the rain was over and gone. (*She's weeping. She smiles as
she weeps.*) I sat down in his shadow with great delight. (*And
she apologises.*) I'm sorry, I'm so sorry. I'm sorry.

And she's gone. (The call over, she becomes a figure / dematerialises.)
Jack *and* **Petra** *have returned. They have heard the very last of the
above.*

Jack   Mum? (*'Was that Mum?'*)

Christopher   Mm! (*A positive 'Mm' to cover his impotence.*)

Jack   How d'you work this thing? (*The telephone-answering
machine.*)

Petra (*angry*)   Just lift the receiver-fucking-thing and dial.
(*She takes charge.*)

Jack (*as* **Petra** *dials*)   His car isn't there.

Christopher   Mm!

Petra   Mum, hi-yih, hi-yih! . . . Yeah, we got your
message just now . . . No, not yet, but we're *sure* to find
him, *certain* . . . Where will you be? . . . And after that? . . .
Gotcha. I'll phone you . . . Mum-Mum-Mum, don't cry,
don't cry, shhhhh . . . *That's* better! Oh, d'you know who we
met? Olivia Morley. She's home, she's back, she's fine, she
said to thank you again for letting her sleep in the spare
room when her father threw her out. For *all* your kindness .
. . She's had it, eight pounds one ounce, she's keeping it! . . .
I'm glad too . . . Guess . . . No-o, I'll give you one more
guess . . . Yeah, a little girl. *Beautiful*, she said . . . Yeah, he's
here, d'you want a word? . . . (*'Well'*) D'you want a word
with Jack? . . . Well, chin up, what-o, whack-o, heigh-ho! –

Here's Jack. (*She hands the phone to* **Jack** *and her anger is back immediately. To herself:*) Gsssss . . .

Jack   Hi . . . Yeah . . . No . . . We had . . . A very *big* meal.

Petra   Has she bloodywell eaten?

Jack   Have you eaten?

Petra   Has she?

Jack   Have you?

Petra   Promise.

Jack   Promise . . . Yeah. Just as soon as . . . yeah, we find him . . . You too. Oh! Dad sends his love and to say how sorry he is about Cornelia . . . Bye.

He feels self-conscious about having spoken for his father; he replaces the phone.

Silence.

Petra   Where to now?

Jack   We've tried everywhere . . . Dad?

Christopher   The Abbey, Monica's new nightclub-hotel-place: I hear he goes there. I'll be with you in a minute.

Jack *and* **Petra** *move aside – as to wait for him outside.*

Christopher, *isolated, has put on his overcoat. (All very brief.) He finds he has a cigarette in one hand; he looks at his other hand: it's empty.*

Christopher   You see: no gun.

He collects up his tape recorder, earphones and some notes and is putting them in his pockets as he leaves:

With confidence.

Jack *and* **Petra** *– and the other figures – follow him. The lights change and disco music, piped, comes up.*

Scene Two

*An ante-room (in what is meant to be a converted gothic building) in
'the Abbey'. Red light and beat music coming from a nightclub type of
bar immediately off it.*

Petra *has gone into the nightclub.* **Jack** *has begun to make up a
song, 'The Man Comes to See Me'; his body is responding to the
music; unconsciously, he is beginning to enjoy the adventure — until
later, when his patience and humour are exceeded.* **Christopher** *is
like a man entering a trap — hell: the red light — but can do nothing
about it.*

Petra *returns, delighted, now magnanimous to* **Christopher** *(and
will continue as such until her generosity is repulsed, later).*

Petra   Found him! Brilliant, brilliant, well done!

Jack   Is he still alive? (*Sniggering at his own wit.*)

Petra   Brill! Anybody got any ten ps? I'll phone Mum.

Petra *and* **Jack**, *in the manner of youngsters, swapping coins.*

Jack   'The man comes to see me, says the trees shimmer.'

Christopher   Did he see you?

Petra   No. The obvious, the Abbey! It's nice, isn't it? (*The
decor.*)

Jack   'The man *he* comes to see me.'

Christopher   Who else is in there?

Petra   Geriatrics! How do we go about getting him home?

Jack   We know, we know! (*Sibling superiority. To*
Christopher:) Will we go in?

Christopher   Ahmm.

Petra   The best thing would be to make and keep the
bastard footless until the morning. Where's the phone? (*She's
moving off.*)

Christopher   Petra! Don't – either of you! – say we were looking for him and we might get him home without a drama.

They nod to his instructions. She beams at him.

Petra   Brilliant! Mum will be pleased. (*She goes.*)

Jack   D'you not want to go in there?

Christopher   Monica has seen us. Don't leave my side tonight, Jack.

Jack   Sure. (*As he moves off:*) Just having a peep. 'The man he comes to see me, says the trees shimmer *red* . . .'

Monica *is joining* **Christopher**. *She's about forty; a laughing, welcoming woman (ideally, big; as generous as she is large). She is remarkably, innocently forthright, and with a capacity to alternate seamlessly and fluently from celebration to concern. It's difficult not to respond to her warmth.*

Monica   Christopher! My *dear*! My dear, my dear, how are you, how are you, how on earth are you!

Christopher   I'm –

Monica   My dear – My *dear* – always lovely to see you!

Christopher   And you.

Monica   Now! And it was only the other day I was saying to Big Dennis we hadn't seen you in an age. But maybe that's because we've moved to our new premises? I hope so. *How* are you, *how* are you!

Christopher   I'm – (a*nd he's pleased to find himself laughing*) – fine! And Dennis?

Monica   Oh Big Dennis, my dear, is! Well, a little depressed. He can't bask in himself, he can't bask in his family. What is the solution? He talks, he dreams about commencing another manner of life and to his quiet astonishment he finds he can't. *Who* is free to play anything but the role allotted? And is that a reason to condemn the

character one was given, to sit in front of the television –
and there's nothing on it? – and he knows it? Male
intelligence. And how is Patricia?

Christopher   Well . . .

Monica   You haven't seen her in a while, I understand.
Jack! My dear – My *dear* – standing back!

Jack (*returning*)   Monica.

Monica   But you're not so slow in other matters. I saw
him the other day, his arm around a gorgeous girl – what's
her name? He's not telling – up by the park – But you didn't
see me – Thursday! But why would you see me: the
beautiful people.

Jack   The place is lovely.

Monica   You like our new premises, Jack?

Jack   It's lovely.

Monica   Well, if banks and building societies can turn
churches into – marketplaces? – might we not in dueness
convert an abbey into a hotel-cum-place-of-relaxation,
keeping as many of the old features as possible of course
and, I can tell you, I can tell you, I am more than happy to
sleep in the abbot's cell down there when Big Dennis's
mystery moods descend. And how is Cornelia?

Christopher (*puzzled that she has not heard about Cornelia*)
Well . . .

Monica   You don't know. Of course. ('*She understands.*')
And the lovely Petra?

Jack   She's here.

Monica   Wonderful! A little reunion! You haven't eaten.
Tck! The kitchen is closed, but wait . . . Yes I can. We had
lovely turbot on this evening and if you would like? . . . I
mean, as you please.

Christopher   Actually –

Monica   No trouble whatsoever. And for Jack?

Jack   Yeah!

Monica   And what about Michael? Soup . . . You're right, Christopher, better that you all have the same thing.

Jack (*to* **Christopher**)   I'll tell him we're here, if you like?

Monica   Do, Jack, do.

Jack *goes into the club.*

Monica   I know why you're here. He's in a state.

Christopher   We'll get him home shortly. (*Laughs.*) Can't force things with our Michael, what! You know Michael.

Monica   I know Michael, but I don't know so much about that – with respect, Christopher.

Christopher   Talking wild, is he? It's a way of life rather than a way of death.

Monica   Killing someone?

Christopher   Everyone talks-thinks about suicide at some time.

Monica   Suicide?

Christopher   . . . He's *not* going to commit suicide?

Monica   He's going to shoot Walter Peters.

Christopher   . . . Who is Walter Peters?

Monica   I don't know.

Christopher (*to himself*)   Walter Peters.

Monica   Walter Peters. Saturday.

Christopher *laughs.*

Monica   Christopher?

Christopher   Nonsense!

Monica   No, my dear. Because when he came in this
evening and showed me the gun. Yes! Like, I would have
dismissed the matter out of hand, but to walk in here like
that? What! When did you see him last?

Christopher   A gun?

Monica   You see! It's been building up. Just look at him!
He's been in here I-don't-know-how-many nights running.
Trying to make him eat – picking at it. Trying to refuse him
drink – you try with your brother. And he's so nice:
gorgeous in his pinstripes last week; this week? – what can
one say?

Christopher   Ahmm.

Monica   But last night, honestly! I tried to persuade him
to stay – number seven, no charge. My dear! ('*The futility of
trying to persuade* **Michael** *of anything.*') I had to call Big
Dennis down – and good enough of him? – he came down
and took the car keys and drove him home and *stayed* with
him for a while, in case, because, as Big Dennis said – mind
you, he didn't have to say it to me – there's something
brewing there, my dear, he said.

Christopher   Being under the strain of Cornelia's –

Monica   Illness for so long, I know, and my heart bleeds
and I'm sorry for interrupting you again, but the child is
really crying wolf.

Christopher   (*wants to tell her – but how to tell her? – that
Cornelia is dead*)   Monica.

Monica   Yes, Christopher, I know: men simply do not
face reality. And I sympathise with your gender, but women
have to do it all the time. He hasn't been near the hospital
to visit her in a week – Are there signs? (I was out there
myself – when was it? She was expecting Patricia – poor
Patricia. But they are so close, sisters, unlike brothers.) I'm
racking my brains to think of what to do but really and truly
I think you are the only one who can stop it.

Christopher   Stop what?

Monica   Stop it happening. Petra! My dear – My *dear* – Another lovely surprise!

Petra (*returning*)   Hi-yih, hi-yih, hi-yih, Monica!

Monica   The lovely attire!

Petra   And yours!

Monica   D'you like it?

Petra   Wow!

They continue to admire each other. While **Christopher**, *to himself:*

Christopher   Stop what happening? (*Turns to* **Jack**, *who is returning:*) He's going to shoot himself, he's going to shoot Walter Peters. Who is Walter Peters?

Jack *doesn't understand. He has returned, a pint of lager in his hand.*

Christopher   Cornelia is dead, isn't she?

Jack (*a silent 'what?' Then:*)   Yeh.

Christopher   He hasn't told Monica about Cornelia.

Jack   He isn't going to do it.

Christopher   I don't know what he's going to do! Is he coming out or what?

Jack   I thought we were going in?

Monica (*hand in hand with* **Petra**, *joining them*)   Wonderful! Now, a little something on the house to take to your table. What would you like, Christopher?

Petra (*protective of him*)   He's off it.

Monica   And is that why we haven't seen you?! Fresh orange juice.

Petra   I'll have a pint of Bud.

Christopher   Could you bring us a bottle of your burgundy.

Monica   Are you sure?

Christopher   Yes, I'm sure.

Monica   Life is short. You try to cut yourself off from the herd but you always come back to us. And Jack is all right for the moment. (*He's got a drink.*) Now, let us find the naughty Michael.

They are moving towards the club. **Christopher** *steeling himself.*

Petra   How is Young Dennis?

Monica *stops – all a bit dramatic – and points a finger at the club (that Young Dennis is in there).* **Jack** *and* **Petra** *go into the club.* **Monica** *holds the increasingly bemused* **Christopher** *back.*

Monica   You are the very man. Do you know, our struggles never cease. Young Dennis, his studies, a blank wall. I have him working in there for the interim. Big Dennis says he had better pull himself together or he's leaving this house. But what about Big Dennis himself?! My dear! And when I don't have to sleep down there in the abbot's cell he's climbing all over and on top of me! And I don't know, is he that interested? But I do my best. And we were thinking if he had someone like you to sit down with him for half an hour. I don't mean tonight, of course.

Christopher   Mmmah! (*Total agreement, though it's likely he doesn't know what she's talking about.*)

Monica   You're very good. We are unhappy married and unmarried we are unhappy. Now let us celebrate it.

They go into the club. Louder music, lights changing, figures moving about again.

Scene Three

A table and table lamp (reminiscent of **Christopher**'s *room) in the deeper light of the club. Nearby, in denser light, figures at a bar — or perhaps the bar is just off. The scene is a bit unreal.*

Christopher *is at the table. He has a bottle of wine.* **Petra** *is with him. She now, like* **Jack**, *has a pint of lager. She's pleased to be with* **Christopher**. *She rolls a cigarette.*

Petra   Those are nice shoes, Dad.

Christopher (*absently*)   Hmm?

Petra   Are they new, Dad? Very nice. I haven't seen nicer on you before.

Christopher   Who are those people with Michael?

Petra   The geriatrics, Dad?

Jack (*coming to join them, singing*)   'So you go for a swim in the stagnant pool.' Monica is bringing him over.

Christopher (*to* **Jack**)   Who are those people with him?

Jack (*shrugs. Then:*)   I'm making up a song. 'And there you see, and there you see . . .'

Christopher   Hmm?

Jack   They're talking about their schoolboy days.

Petra   Ger-i-atric wankers.

Jack   The terrible things that used to happen to them at school, forty years ago.

Christopher   In the playground?

Jack   Yeh.

Petra   D'you want a rollie, Dad?

Christopher   In the playground, in the schoolyard? (*A degree of urgency to* **Jack**, *to elaborate.*)

Jack   Yeh. 'And-there-you-see' – *mermaids*!

Petra   Piss-art-ists. Want it, Dad? (*The rollie.*)

Christopher (*turns on her*)   Why aren't you at home with your mother?

Petra (*affronted; her gesture repulsed*)   . . . I could ask the same of you, couldn't I?

Christopher   I asked you a question!

Petra   She's out! You know: out? I phoned! You know: the telephone?

Christopher (*to* **Jack**)   Yes?

Petra   Geessssstupid! (*She moves away, to sit / stand at a remove from them.*)

Christopher (*to* **Jack**)   Yes?!

Jack   She was holding out a hand to you.

Christopher   Schooldays – schoolboys – schoolyards – the terrible things that used to happen to them: is that what they're talking about?

Jack   Yeh.

Christopher   Bullies?

Jack *nods.* (*'Is my father going loopy?'*)

Christopher   Aaa! Wally. Walter Peters. It's all making sense! (*He laughs, he drinks.*)

Petra (*from her remove*)   I just didn't want to miss the fun!

Michael *and retinue are coming from the bar.* **Michael** *is laughing, messing with* **Monica**, *grinning into her ear ('Monica, do I love you?'), his arm around her: a glass of whiskey in his other hand.* **Geoffrey** *and* **Tony** *follow for a little, briefly, before returning to the bar.*

Michael *is a handsome man, elegant, late forties. (Perhaps a little emaciated.) But he's been drinking for a few days. His suit is rumpled,*

*he's probably slept in it. His impeccable manners under other conditions
are not entirely absent. But swings of mood: boyish charm, suspicion,
moroseness, hilarity; laughter perversely expressing pain; a man who
would like to smash his glass, but doesn't.*

Michael   Monica, do I love you? –

Monica   Michael, Michael, stop it, stop it! Oh dear – My
dear – Unhand me! Be good! Look at who we have over here
for you! Michael is the great old flirt.

Michael, *in this first moment, sees* **Christopher** *as some kind of
long-lost friend and comes to him expansively.*

Michael   Christopher!

Christopher   I'm sorry about –

Michael *(now recognising him, he wheels about, rejecting*
Christopher *and the outstretched hand)*   Fucking brother!

Monica   Jack, another chair over here for your uncle!

Michael   Jack! What precisely – exactly! – is our
relationship?

Monica   Come now, Michael, sit over here.

Michael   Jack!

Jack   Friends!

Michael   Friends! Did you hear, everybody?!

Monica   Now, sit down, Michael.

Michael   This calls for a celebration. (To **Christopher**:)
What are you having?

Christopher   I've got a drink.

Michael *(suspiciously)*   Pardon?

Christopher *(shows him the bottle of wine)*   I'm fine.

Michael   And is everyone else a leper? Jack, speak up!

Jack   Pint!

Michael   Three large whiskeys!

Monica   And is it serious, Jack, that gorgeous girl?

Michael   Monica, three large –

Monica   He won't tell us her name, Michael.

Jack   I don't know her name.

Michael   Pardon?

Monica   Where is she from then?

Jack   Frankfurt.

Michael   Frankfurt! Grrrrrr, good at English, Jack, is she? Jack takes after his uncle Michael.

Christopher   Jack does *not* take after his uncle Michael.

Michael   Pardon? (*Suspicious again; his eyes fixed on* **Christopher**. *Then:*) I'm not going home.

Christopher *affects a shrug and sits.*

Michael (*laughs*)   Friends! Monica, do I love you?

Monica   You do, Michael – Now asparagus soup for three and three turbots. (*She has cutlery for the table.*)

Michael   What's this? ('*What's the cutlery for?*')

Monica   Oh and what about Petra? –

Michael   What-is-this?!

Monica   Asparagus –

Michael   No food!

Monica   Soup of the day –

Michael   Are we friends?

Monica   You haven't eaten for –

Michael   Do you respect a hunger-striker?

Monica   Stop being tragic now.

Michael   Do you respect the rights of man, do you respect
– I ask you! – a hunger-striker?

Jack (*to* **Christopher**)   Tell her it's OK.

Michael   Since there are no other bloody rights.

Jack   'We've eaten.' (To **Christopher**, *meaning 'Tell her'*.)

Michael   Well, Michael has that right.

Christopher   We're fine, Monica.

Michael   Pardon? Settled. The man of letters has spoken.

Monica *nods/winks at* **Christopher** *and leaves.*

Michael (*calls*)   And thank you, Monica! That woman
would strip well, what? Cheers! Wouldn't she, Christopher?

Christopher   Cheers. (*They drink.*)

Petra, *at a remove from them – excluded – is concerned for*
Michael. *She is also pursuing her own tactic of getting him 'footless'*
and she goes purposefully to the bar.

Christopher   . . . But isn't there something we have to
talk about?

Michael   And I heard about what you did to Chokki.

Christopher   Michael –

Michael   Man's-best-friend. I ask you, Mummy's dog!
Did you hear, everybody?

Christopher   That is neither here nor there, we have
something to –

Michael   Why'd you do it?! Why-did-you-do-it! Neither
here nor?! I met a vet! If I had known you were going to do
such a thing! Bloody Christopher. Does he have any
feelings? Jack?

Jack   You were offered the dog.

Michael   Sorry, Jack?

Jack   You were offered . . . (*He gestures the rest of it.*)

Petra *returns during this and stands by with a glass of whiskey, waiting her chance.*

Michael   I do not have a spare room for a fucking dog! What would Mummy have said?! Jack?! No point in asking him.

Jack (*to* **Christopher**)   Isn't it against college rules to keep a dog in –

Michael   She would have said – dreadful. That is what she would have, Jack, said.

Petra   It's sad, Uncle Michael, but –

Michael   She would have, Christopher, written another novel. Your grandmother, Jack, Mummy. (*She*) Didn't like him. Two geniuses, I suppose, couldn't live in the same house. That is what she would have, Christopher, said.

Petra's *chance has arrived. She takes the empty glass out of* **Michael**'s *hand and replaces it with her glass of whiskey.*

Petra   It's sad, Uncle Michael, but Chokki was old.

Michael (*absently*)   It's what, love? (*Note: It's doubtful if* **Michael** *recognises/registers* **Petra** *as* **Petra** *in this scene.*)

Jack (*to* **Christopher**)   And she was eating the furniture, wasn't she?

Michael   I do not bloody care what she was eating! It is a dog's nature to eat college furniture!

Christopher   And it's my nature to put her down if she does!

Michael   . . . Good grief! Did you hear that? (*Asking* **Jack** *to share his disbelief.*)

Jack   No! (*His solidarity with* **Christopher**.)

Michael   The man is an idiot.

Christopher   There is a matter of urgency we have to talk about –

Michael   A donkey –

Christopher   Michael –

Michael   Corridors of learning for you! Golden letters after their names, rounded humps from carrying all they know. But you mark my words, one of these days a golden stiletto in the back from one of your colleagues will soon pull your shoulder blades back together again. (*And he drinks his whiskey. And sighs.*)

Jack   Ask him about the arrangements.

Christopher (*gestures to **Jack** not to interfere*)   Michael, I have to go soon.

Michael *sighs heavily again to himself.*

Christopher   I've work to do.

Michael (*wearily*)   And I suppose I shall be phoning everybody in the morning to apologise.

Christopher   And your apology will be accepted, but now we must talk about –

Michael (*revived, attacking again*)   Why should you accept it, why should you? D'you see what I mean, everybody? A donkey!

Petra *goes purposefully to the bar again.*

Michael   You know absolutely, Christopher, *nothing*. I'm the one who has discovered things: Michael. Meaning of life? Answer, please? All you've done is made an unholy botch of things – without even knowing it! And a shambles of the lives of those about you. The meaning of life: the spirit and the flesh. The flesh? – How many women have you screwed in your life, Jack, your entire life – usefully? No point in asking him. (*To **Christopher**:*) All you have only ever had, are your wife, and mine, and Monica, I suppose.

So, you see! And the spirit? God is up there, isn't he? What-is-he-doing up there? Answer, please? I'm down here. D'you see what I mean? So, you see: what more is there to say? (*Morosely, to himself:*) Enough is enough.

Petra (*returns, and puts another glass of whiskey into his hand*) Drink hearty!

Jack   He's indulging himself.

Christopher (*perversely sitting back in his chair*)   No!

Michael (*absently, morosely, sighing*)   That's love, thanks, love, cheers. (*And he drinks.*)

Jack   He's –

Christopher   No, this is most constructive! Cheers, everybody!

Monica (*coming in, professionally*)   And how are we getting along here? Wonderful! Jack, I haven't forgotten you: your drink on the house when you've finished that one. Oh, and, Christopher, that little matter we were discussing?

Christopher   Mmmah!

Monica   I'm taking steps. (*She nods/winks and goes out again.*)

Jack *has moved aside to* **Petra**.

Jack   They're indulging themselves.

Petra   Bastards.

Jack   Where are you getting the whiskey?

Petra   Young Dennis in there.

Jack   I'm starving.

Both of them are aware that **Geoffrey** *and* **Tony** *have put in another appearance (to check on* **Michael** *from a distance).* **Jack** *sees potential danger in them.*

I think we should get out of here now.

Petra   I'll try the phone again for Mum. (*She goes.*)

Tony   Girlie? Girlie? (*Calling to her; plaintive, foolish – like a cat.*)

Geoffrey (*who has returned to the bar, off*)   Tony!

Tony   Geoffrey! Oft in the stilly night! (*He has gone off again, too.*)

Michael   I took a year off – sabbatical, Christopher?

Christopher   Ah!

Michael   Where's Jack?

Jack   Here I am!

Michael   Permanent fucking sabbatical, Jack, as far as I am concerned.

Christopher   Dropping out?

Jack   Let's go somewhere else!

Michael   Party, Jack?

Jack   Yeah! – Where's your coat?

Michael *stands to point to somewhere off –* **Jack** *goes off for the coat – and to finish his drink.*

Michael   Finish this. (*Drinks. And:*) Yes, Christopher: dropping out. But when Michael says dropping out he means business. But you don't know what I'm talking about. South America?

Christopher   Saturday?

Michael   Pardon?

Christopher   Suicide, South America?

Michael   What on earth are you –

Christopher   Walter Peters? (*All mock-casually.*)

Michael *starts laughing, laughing at length, laughing and coughing, highly amused.*

Michael   Do you remember *him*?!

Christopher   Oh yes.

Michael   Wally!

Christopher   Oh yes.

Jack*, returning with* **Michael***'s overcoat, meets* **Petra***, who is returning from the phone.*

Jack   Did you get through to Mum?

She didn't. **Jack***, through the following, succeeds in getting* **Michael** *into the overcoat: quite a business.*

Michael (*laughing*)   At school?! – Wally, Walter Peters! – Do you?!

Christopher   Yes.

Jack   Coat, Michael.

Michael   He picked on the brilliant Christopher too?!

Christopher   You, though a slob, were the brilliant one.

Jack   Coat, Michael, here we are –

Michael   Why'd he pick on you?

Christopher   I was innocent of the charge. Why'd he pick on you?

Michael   Prank? Called him a bollix? An anonymous letter to his childhood sweetheart's mother? It didn't take much in those good old days to incur the awful wrath of Walter, did it?

Christopher   His tyranny, in those good old days, outdistanced God's.

Michael   I saw him walking in the street two days ago: a white suit – *white*, I ask you, Jack! Wally! (*Points:*) Going into the pink house down there – *pink*, I ask you, Christopher! I thought he was dead or at least had gone abroad, but you cannot mistake an ox. We ready, Jack?

Jack   Yeah!

Michael   Party!

Jack   Yeah! (*Takes his arm and begins leading him off.*)

Christopher   Excuse me? (*Continues seated.*) When is the funeral?

Michael   Someone say something?

Jack   Let's go, everybody!

Christopher   When is the funeral?

Jack (*aside to* **Christopher**)   Let's get him out of here first.

Christopher   No-no-no –

Jack   He's ready to go.

Christopher   No, I'm enjoying this.

Michael   Is this – private conversation?

Jack   Michael –

Christopher   When is the funeral?

Michael   When is?

Christopher   When is the funeral?

Michael   *What* fucking funeral?! Sorry, Jack, you wanted to – (To **Christopher**:) There are fucking funerals every day of the week! I beg your pardon, Jack, you wanted to say?

Christopher   What about the arrangements for the funeral?

Michael   And! – Christopher? – In my opinion – I ask a simple question! – Is that any of your fucking business? (*And turns again to* **Jack**:) Sorry, Jack?

Christopher   It has been *made* my business, unfortunately.

Geoffrey and **Tony** *have re-emerged.* **Jack** *has registered them.*

Jack   Dad, let's go –

Christopher   Be quiet!

Michael (*to* **Christopher**)   Pardon? – (*To* **Jack**:) Pardon?

Jack (*offended, sits down/gives up; shrugs*)   How're things?

Christopher   We understand how you must feel, but –

Michael   How are? – (*To* **Christopher**:) Pardon? – (*To* **Jack**:) *Things*? (*To* **Christopher**:) Did you hear that?! (*He's now trying to get out of his overcoat.*) That is worse than –

Christopher   I've work to do, I must go soon –

Michael   Worse than – the piped music she uses here!

Geoffrey   You ride shotgun, Tony son.

Geoffrey and **Tony** *join the scene.*

Geoffrey *is seventy – or thereabouts. Physically, he can carry his drink, but it induces a romantic nonsense. Sober, he is an everyday, decent businessman.*

Tony *is forty. He's in business with* **Geoffrey**. *He isn't at all bright; there isn't much of a difference, if any, when he's sober; really, he doesn't understand his own catchphrases: they come out automatically or are barked in response to his name. An innocence that can be physically threatening; a stocky, muscular frame; perhaps a bright pullover under his jacket with a paunch in the middle. He probably still plays club rugby.*

Geoffrey   Everything OK, pal? Because we're just in here.

Michael   I beg your pardon?

Geoffrey   Tony!

Tony   A dry finger can't lick salt!

Geoffrey   Who are your friends?

Michael   What is he talking about?

Geoffrey   These guys, pal.

Jack   Who are you?

Geoffrey   Checking it out for you, Mike.

Michael   Did you not hear the young gentleman request your credentials?

Geoffrey   Geoff Williams. ('*Wyatt Earp*') Casing matters, Mike.

Michael   Casing Matters Mike – What on earth is he?!

Geoffrey   Understood, amigos?

Michael   Piss off!

Geoffrey   Understood, amigo. We're in here. Tony!

Tony   You supply the birds, we'll provide the cages!

And they return to the bar.

Michael   *In there?* (*He is wrestling with his coat again to get out of it.*) Two minutes, Jack: Gents.

Monica (*comes in, a pint of lager for* **Jack**)   Now, Jack!

Michael   Monica, who is that man?

Monica (*helps* **Michael** *out of his coat / takes it from him*) Geoffrey. You have been with him all afternoon and evening and Tony.

Michael   I know I've been with him all afternoon and evening and Tony: what does he mean he's 'in there'? (*He goes off to the Gents*:) Bloody hell.

Petra   Is there a window in the loo? I don't trust him.

Jack *follows* **Michael** *off.* **Monica**, *who has been ostensibly dusting down* **Michael**'s *coat, calls* **Christopher** *aside for a private word.*

Monica   Christopher?

Christopher   Mmmah! (*Joining her.*)

Monica   Only be a moment, Petra sweetheart!

Petra   Not at all, Monica love! (*Inwardly fuming at this further exclusion.*)

Monica   Is the wine to your liking? (*She produces a gun from underneath* **Michael***'s coat.*) You see! In his pocket. I put a rubber-toy thing of Young Dennis's from the attic in its place: the state he is in he won't know the difference.

Christopher (*alarmed*)   My father's.

Monica   Honestly, I wouldn't sleep.

Christopher   He was a lieutenant-colonel in the war.

Monica   I mean, if one does the right thing in taking a person's car keys?

Christopher   I took his fob watch as a memento, Michael took that.

Monica   It probably doesn't work but to be on the safe side. Here.

Christopher   I don't want it.

Monica   Christopher?

Christopher   What do I do with it?

Monica   I don't know . . . Put it away.

Christopher *takes it. Clumsily, to get it to fit in his pocket, he has to take out his tape recorder.*

Monica   Now I can breathe.

Jack (*returning; to* **Petra**)   He can't escape, there's no window in there.

Monica (*leaving*)   Quite, quite lovely, my dears – my *dears* – to see you all!

Christopher *is left isolated, tape recorder in his hand, the gun in his pocket.*

Petra (*for* **Christopher**'s *benefit*)   Two girls, Jack – children – from my school attempted suicide last year!

Jack   What?

Petra   Both of them are permanently damaged!

Jack   Take it easy.

Petra (*daintily*)   Fuck! Five girls – I know them personally – have done that trip to London for that little operation.

Jack   Take it easy –

Petra   Some of them didn't come back! Will you excuse me? I shall now try phoning Mum again. (*She goes off.*) Fuck!

Christopher *returns to the table.* **Jack** *smiles a gentle smile, indicating the departed* **Petra**, *hoping* **Christopher** *will find her personality simply amusing.*

Christopher   Is there something funny?

Jack   . . . No! . . . She's trying to help . . . She's –

Christopher   Jack, Jack, I've a lot on my mind, we've never had a row as far as I remember and if at all possible could we avoid one now?

Jack *nods to the sense of this.*

Christopher   You were saying?

Jack   Petra. She doesn't hate you. (*Gentle smile.*) Neither do I. She's been fighting Mum's battle.

Christopher   What battle?

Jack   You walked out.

Christopher   What battle?

Jack   I watched and heard the rows! You walked out six months ago, you left.

Christopher   Consigned you to anonymity and
illegitimacy?

Jack   Is that another quotation?

Christopher (*points after* **Petra**)   Her language, her
staying out late, her – sixteen years of age! – how many of
those things – pints! – does she drink?

Jack   Everyone's doing it!

Christopher   Because they're fighting their mothers'
battles?

Jack   You walked out! Look, I'm only saying – I'm a man
too, you know?

Christopher   Your mother and I agreed –

Jack   She didn't agree, you agreed! To start your new life,
pursue your whatever. But it's reprehensible to deny the
truth. You know?

Christopher   Oh? Reprehensible.

Jack   OK. The reprehensible thing then is not that you
walked out or that you deny it but that you did it to bury
your head deeper in a *book*, and that makes no sense to me.

Christopher (*turns away*)   I don't have to listen to – (*Turns
back:*) You've let *me* down: I'm disappointed in *you*. You're
aimless, dressed in rags, no job. And, like everyone else, you
blame me for it. You've caused me great sorrow, Jack –
you're all punishing me. You have caused me woe.

Jack   These aren't rags!

Christopher   You're the one who walks out on things.

Jack   You're facing them – in *Trinity*? University has
nothing to do with life.

Christopher   This after the two terms you spent there?

Jack   Yes.

Christopher   You will publish your findings no doubt?

Jack   And! From the general to the specific, the very best way to stop thinking is to become a philosopher – or shoot yourself in the head! (*He regrets it. But he has been hurt too . . . A silent gesture of apology. Then:*) You're pressed for time: I understand: Petra and I have it in hand now: *we'll* get him home.

Christopher   No! I finish things, Jack, people can depend on me –

Jack   I only said –

Christopher   I'm not a parasite, I don't tell lies. When I say I'm going to do a thing I see it through, not like you, for better or worse . . . (*He turns away, he can't do anything right, he's caught in a nightmare. Hand to his pocket, the gun is there; to his other pocket, finds the cigarette; toys with it.*)

Jack   . . . D'you want to light that thing? . . . Dad?

Christopher   No, I don't want to light that thing! (*And, like a man of action, he pulls his earphones out of a pocket and switches on his tape recorder.*)

Christopher's recorded voice   But whereas other philosophers declare that the world as phenomenon is known to us, they assert that the numenon, that is, the *Ding an sich*, is unknown. Schopenhauer, however, maintains that it is known . . . (*Etc., if required: 'Indeed, far from being unknown, it is known to Schopenhauer as a unitary principle. And he calls his principle will.'*)

Geoffrey, *the sheriff, has come in during this.*

Geoffrey   Everything OK in here?

Christopher *plugs in his earphones, thus terminating his recorded voice and sits, listening to his tape in private.* **Geoffrey** *notices* **Michael**'s *absence.*

Geoffrey   Mike? (*To* **Jack**:) Hey, where's Mike?

Jack   Fuck off.

Tony (*entering, following* **Petra**)   Girlie?

Petra   Fuck off.

Jack   Did you get through to Mum?

Petra   Yeh. Get him out of the loo.

Jack *collects* **Michael**'s *overcoat and is heading for the Gents. But* **Geoffrey** *and* **Tony** *feel that they have been insulted.*

Geoffrey   Tony!

Tony (*excited, stays* **Jack** *with an upraised hand and indicates that the room is now an arena for battle*)   No problem! Geoffrey: was it sonny here or four-ears over there? (*He decides to deal with 'four-ears',* **Christopher**.) Want to play ball, friend? . . . I've had two trials on the possibles for my country! You? (*'How many trials have you had?'*) Compared with rugby, boxing is a puff's game! (*He's running out of ideas.*) . . . Stand up! (*Tips of his fingers under* **Christopher**'s *arm, he assists* **Christopher** *to rise.*) . . . It's the highest body-contact sport! . . . Multiply mass by acceleration and what've you got? Rugby! (*He doesn't know what his next move should be.*) . . . Take off the earphones.

Christopher, *petrified, obeys. And:*

Christopher's recorded voice   So: The body is the appearance, the phenomenon, of which the will, that is the *Ding an sich*, is the reality. And the focus of the will lies in the reproductive system. Sex. Now: sex and the sexual drive –

This has taxed **Tony**'s *mind, momentarily. Now he takes the recorder and, not knowing what else to do with it, he throws it away. And:*

Tony   Your play, friend!

A movement from **Jack** *to catch/field the recorder, but it's gone (possibly out of a window). Immediately following,* **Petra** *intervenes herself between* **Tony** *and* **Christopher** – *to protect* **Christopher**.

Petra (*face to face with* **Tony**)   You bloodywell person! You extremely bloodywell stupid person! Do you want to hit someone? Do you?! Hit me then, go on, I dare you, hit me!

A mêlée has started. (*The following is all one fluent action.*) **Jack** *has joined in* –

Jack (*swinging* **Michael**'s *coat at* **Tony** *and* **Geoffrey**) Hey! Hey! Hey! –

All become involved, in ways appropriate to character.

Geoffrey   Run with it, Tony!

Tony   No problem! –

Geoffrey   Heel, heel! –

Petra *is swept aside and comes unceremoniously sprawling out of it.* (*Out of what looks like a scrum?*) **Jack** *is grappling with* **Tony** –

Petra   Gsssss . . . !

Geoffrey   Take him down, Tony son!

Tony   No problem! –

Christopher *watches horrified. And* **Michael** *is making a staggering, joyful, expansive return:*

Michael   Geoffrey! Tony! Amigos!

Geoffrey   Step aside, Mike, leave it to Tony!

Jack *now has* **Tony** *in a neck-hold, rendering* **Tony** *ineffective providing he does not release him* –

Geoffrey   Aw, down him, Tony, take him down!

Tony (*half-strangled voice*)   No problem.

Christopher   Let him go, Jack.

Jack   Jesus, let him go?!

Michael   My coat! (*His coat is being trampled on.*)

Petra   Beat the shit out of him, Jack!

Geoffrey   The blind side, Tony!

Tony   No prob – (*He's choking.*)

Michael (*retrieving his coat*)   Bloody hell! Bloody hell!

Geoffrey   Aw, wheel him!

Petra   Take his fucking head off!

Michael (*dusting his coat*)   Dreadful! Dreadful!

Monica (*coming in*)   What is going on? Boys, boys, boys!

Michael (*searching his pockets*)   Car keys, anybody?

Monica   *Boys*! What a din!

Geoffrey   Foul language, insulting behaviour –

Petra   Get the bloodywell pig!

Monica   Petra! My dear – My *dears*! Geoffrey, Tony –

Geoffrey   We were having a quiet drink in there –

Petra   Oh yes, oh yes, a quiet drink –

Monica   A family reunion, Geoffrey!

Geoffrey   Eh?

Monica   A little family get-together! A father and his children and their uncle.

Geoffrey   Jack son, Tony son –

Monica   Geoffrey and Tony: two of our regulars, businessmen down from the North on business, Geoffrey-and-Tony, G-and-T!

During the above, **Michael** *– searching for his car keys – finds something in his pocket that puzzles him. It looks like a gun but it doesn't work, it even bends – 'Bloody hell!' – and when he throws it on the floor it bounces – 'Good grief!' . . . And, unobserved by the others, he leaves – 'Dreadful!'*

Geoffrey   Family confab, Tony, Jack son, let him go.

Jack   I'm letting you go now. (*Releases him.*)

Monica   My *dears!*

Tony   No problem.

Monica, **Geoffrey** *and* **Tony** *go to the bar or they retire a little.* (**Monica**: *'a family reunion'*, **Geoffrey**: *'all a mistake'*, **Tony**: *'family confab'*.)

Jack, *adrenalin going, is moving about, sing-songing* 'The man he comes to see me, says the trees shimmer red —' *He sees the stunned (?)* **Christopher** *and shouts angrily at him:*

Jack   'Was that necessary?' – Still disappointed in me? – I've let you down again? – Petra didn't make another gesture to you?

While **Petra** *has registered* **Michael**'s *absence: she circles the room, looking this way and that for him. She comes to a stop.*

Petra   So now, the bastard's gone! Shhhit! Jack! (*'Follow me.'*) Shit. (*The last, daintily, as she goes.*)

Jack *follows, to search for* **Michael**.

Monica *sees them leave and follows enquiringly.* **Geoffrey** *and* **Tony** *follow* **Monica**.

Music up, lights down to a single light, the table lamp. We are back in **Christopher**'s *room. He has a cigarette in one hand, a gun in the other.*

Scene Four

Christopher, *isolated, stands watching the scene. It could be a deserted street or a deserted parking lot: the pathetic figure of* **Michael** *moves along it. He appears lost and he is crying to himself. He comes to a halt. He is literally twisted in pain (from repressed grief more than from drink).*

The others arrive gradually: **Petra** *and* **Jack**, *then* **Monica**, *then* **Geoffrey** *and* **Tony** . . . *And* **Petra** *comes forward, approaching* **Michael**, *cautiously, caring.*

Petra   Uncle Michael?

Michael   Can't find my car, love.

Petra   Uncle Michael?

Michael   Can't even find my car keys.

Petra   It's all right, it's all right. But you're going home now, aren't you? Uncle Michael?

Michael (*looks at her; a slow dawning*)   . . . Petra. Where on earth did you . . . (*'come out of'*)? I haven't seen you in . . . (*'months'*)!

Petra   Oho!

Laughing-crying, he embraces her.

Michael   Darling little niece.

Petra   Darling Uncle Michael.

Michael   Little tittle titties growing.

Petra   Now now, Uncle . . . *Uncle*!

Michael (*clenched, pained face*)   Come home with me.

Petra   Oho, oho, gerron.

She eases him to arm's length, holding both of his hands, to circle with him, as one might with a child, in a game, a slow dance.

I just wanted to see you . . . To look at you . . . To behold you . . . To say how much I love you . . . And Cornelia . . . And that you're going to be all right . . . Aren't you? Uncle Michael? . . . Because you mean so much to us . . . Because we are so precious to each other, because we love one another so much.

He has sunk to his knees, in tears at her feet, his arms around her legs. She strokes his hair.

There there, there there . . . (*She assists him up.*) And you have something to tell us before you go home with Jack, haven't you? Uncle Michael?

He nods.

Monica   Cornelia: Is she? (*Her hand to her mouth.*)

Petra   . . . Nite-nite, everybody! Nite!

She has to leave. (Hides in the shadows.) The tears she's been restraining all day, all night, are about to break. **Christopher***'s eyes follow her.*

Monica (*to herself*)   Oh dear. Oh my dear.

Geoffrey   Misunderstanding.

Tony   Misunderstanding.

Monica   If there's anything at all that we can do.

Geoffrey   When is the funeral, Mike?

Michael (*doesn't know, but he's good for a tragic line*)   I stand before you a widower and childless.

Geoffrey   We'll be there.

Monica   She sang at my wedding. (*She leaves.*)

Geoffrey   Tony.

Tony (*shaking hands with* **Jack**)   Keep in touch.

Jack *leaves with* **Michael**. **Geoffrey** *and* **Tony** *follow* **Monica**.

Christopher*'s eyes on the shadowy place. Now we hear* **Petra** *weeping.* **Christopher** *approaches, cautiously, caring.*

Christopher   . . . Petra?

Petra *emerges. The child-woman explodes, circling him, spitting it at him through her tears:*

Petra   Did I get pregnant, did I commit suicide, did I have to go away to have an abortion? Did I get my Junior

Cert, will I get my Leaving – Does any of it matter – Does anything matter to you but *you*? Will I drop out of college, will I drop out of life, will I walk out on my family when I have them, will I know how to be a parent? *Man!* Do I know the meaning of trust-trust-trust? Big deal, the man of letters, the speech-maker, the professor! Oh! And Jack – Jack-Jack-Jack – is gone off that way for you! You shit! You nothing! . . . Mum is at home now. Nite!

She's gone. He is still, head bowed. (Figures appearing?) 'O Silver Moon' from Rusalka *by Dvořák.*

Scene Five

A table, a table lamp and **Maud**, *seated, posed, watching her reflection in a cheval mirror. She's about sixty; a sad, elegant anachronism in dress and lost dreams. (Apart from once, at the end of the scene when she looks at* **Christopher** *directly, she looks at the mirror; the pitch at which she holds her head acknowledges the person she is addressing. And it does not appear to matter that* **Christopher** *does not answer her questions; it's as if she knows the answers.) On a record player (which we don't have to see): 'O Silver Moon'; she has a remote control for adjusting the volume, as she requires, and for switching off and on.*

At a second table and table lamp, **Christopher** *is sitting, a glass of port in one hand, the gun in the other in his lap.*

Maud   . . . She is singing to the moon . . . because she has fallen in love with the handsome prince, who came to bathe in the limpid pool, her home . . . she longs for a mortal body, in order that she might know the warmth of union with him . . . to share the wonder of life with a human being . . . Are you married?

Christopher   . . . Is that you? (*'Singing'*)

Maud   No. Because then, for very good reason, I stopped . . . And her wish is granted. But there is a condition. If he

proves false, both she and he will be damned for ever . . .
The decision is irrevocably taken . . . Do you love her?

Christopher . . . Does he keep guns? (*He holds up the gun.*)

Maud No. You are quite safe . . . He won't be much
longer. He likes to look neat without being helped.

Christopher Sorry?

Maud He has a bad ear for music. But he's proud of his
memory . . . And she leaves the limpid pool, her home, to
love her prince and be loved in return.

Wally (*off*) . . . Wo-ho-ho, wo-ho-ho!

Maud That will be Walter now.

Christopher *stands, nervously, gun behind his back.*

Wally *comes (careering?) in in a wheelchair. He doesn't need a
wheelchair but it stands him greater odds, he reckons, against being shot
by callers. Mostly, he affects to be quadriplegic; 'Ouch!' or 'Arrrgh!'
when he realises he has moved a limb too much, dropped the pretence.
Blazer-and-cravat type or maybe an off-white game-hunter's kind of
tunic. He's younger than* **Maud**. *Practically everything he says is an
exclamation. He's too hearty-sounding by half. He is terrified.*

Christopher's *underlying emotional state and confusion are not
helped by* **Wally**'s *wheelchair.*

Wally Wo-ho-ho, wo-ho-ho, talking about me, someone
talking about me?! (*He brakes to a halt.*) Catalani, Maud? Cat-
a-lani?! Is this the way to entertain a guest? Switch'm off,
switch'm off! Bloody Catalani. (**Maud** *switches off the music.*)
That's better! Old boy, old boy, good of you to call, good of
you to call! What?! Don't get up, no need to stand! Good of
you to call, I appreciate, I do, good of you to call! What's
that? (*Did* **Christopher** *say something?*) . . . Nothing! To be
sure! (*He didn't say anything and that's perfect.*) Long time. Long
time? Long time. And! . . . She give you nothing stiffer
than?! Ouch! (*To* **Maud**:) Get up! (*To* **Christopher**.) T'be
sure yeh will, t'be sure yeh will, won't take no for an – (*To*

Maud:) Get up! Cognac, whiskey, this's an old friend, wo-ho-ho!

Christopher This is fine.

Wally Eh?

Christopher No.

Wally If y'say so, if y'say so, if that's yer tipple, if that's yer choice. It's what I drink m'self. (*To* **Maud**:) Get up! Haven't much say in these things now, since my – (*Taps his legs. Then:*) Ouch! Arrrgh! My ration, Maud.

While **Maud** *holds a glass of port to* **Wally**'s *lips,* **Christopher** *sits, stands, sits . . . Inner agitation. The gun is visible in his hand, yet no one comments on it.*

Wally (*to* **Maud**) Enough! . . . So! So! How're things, how're – Good? Good! Good! So things're good, things're good, good of you to call! Hang about, elephant's brain: Christopher.

Christopher Yesss.

Wally Eh? . . . Hang about, younger brother, don't tell me his name.

Christopher Michael.

Wally I would've got it! Ouch! . . . Yes?

Christopher, *fixed on* **Wally**, *shakes his head, absently.*

Wally Been back that ways since?

Christopher Ahmmm . . .

Wally (*to* **Maud**, *who has moved; terrified that she will leave the room*) Where you off to? Sit! She's like a hen. Been back that ways since, Christopher?

Christopher Yesss, no.

Wally Y'have?

Christopher No.

Wally   Remember the beak?

Christopher   No –

Wally   Y'do, y'do! The headmaster, was fond of you –

Christopher   I don't –

Wally   Y'do –

Christopher   I don't –

Wally   Y'do! – You cared for him a lot!

Christopher   I don't!

Wally   . . . Top him up, Maud.

Christopher   I don't, Wally. (*To* **Maud**:) No, thank you.

Wally (*to* **Maud**)   Up, get up! (*To* **Christopher**:) Y'don't mind if I do?

Christopher (*to himself*)   I never cared for anyone.

And, while **Maud** *feeds* **Wally** *another sip of port, he starts to pace (?), the gun held tight against his body.*

Wally (*eyes screwed sideways, watching* **Christopher**, *whispers to* **Maud**)   Enough. Sit . . . (*And to* **Christopher** *when he comes to a halt*:) Eh?

Christopher   I called about a matter.

Wally   And that brother of yours – Bit of a lad, what?!

Christopher   I called about – ahmmm! –

Wally   But weren't we all, weren't we all! –

Christopher   A matter that has started to bother me.

Wally   Boys will be boys!

Christopher   . . . But, aren't you surprised, I called rather late.

Wally   So what? Ouch!

Christopher   It's two o'clock in the morning.

Wally   Lights were on, Maud sits up, what're old friends for?!

Christopher   . . . And I'm surprised that . . .

Wally   Yes? (*Aside to* **Maud**:) Chip in.

Maud   And he's surprised that you're not surprised to see him, Walter.

Wally   Surprised?! – No! – I mean I'm – Yes! If he says so!

Maud   And *he* (*meaning* **Wally**) is surprised at where you found our address.

Wally   Immaterial! – Not at all! – But if, y'know?! ('*If he wishes to tell us*')

Christopher   The book.

Wally   We're not in it.

Christopher   You are.

Wally   If y'say so – but we're not in it. Maud – ex – chip in.

Maud   We are ex-directory. Because when we returned from abroad, Walter had two other callers –

Wally   Eh?

Maud   Old school friends too, come to call late at night, like you. So Walter had us removed from the book.

Wally   Kind of people to call on me, Christopher?

Christopher   No. (*To himself; it doesn't explain matters.*)

Maud   Perhaps it was a very old directory.

Wally   There – she has it – mystery solved – First sensible thing y've said in yer life! I bet you've nothing like her at home? (*He taps his head, meaning* **Maud** *has a screw loose, then is about to go 'Ouch!' but* **Christopher** *is buried in himself.*)

Short silence. Short as it is, it becomes too much for **Wally**.

Oh, put on the bloody Catalani again, I know that's all yer itching for.

Maud   Dvořák, Walter.

Wally   Dvořák, Catalani, elephant's brain but I keep mixing the twisters up.

Maud   Do you mind hearing it again?

Christopher (*absently*)   No.

Wally   Where are you, oh where are you my beloved – same old thing.

Christopher *looks at him; fixes on him.*

Wally   Eh? . . . Music man yourself, Christopher? . . . Work going well? . . . I'm retired – you retired? – I'm retired.

Christopher   Yesss, yesss.

Wally   Eh?

Christopher   And I'm surprised at that.

Wally   Which – What?

Christopher   *That*, the wheelchair – Recent?

Wally (*taps the chair*)   This?

Christopher   Yesss!

Wally   No! Funniest thing, comes and goes. (*He half stands – with a touch of 'watch me, no hands' – to demonstrate his point, and sits again.*) Neurological stuff, the experts tell me.

'O Silver Moon' again. (Or the resumption of it.) And **Maud** *is talking to the mirror again.*

Maud   How warm and gentle her kisses . . . How she tries to speak to him with her eyes, so that he might learn to live.

Wally   Fish out of water, what! . . .

Maud   . . . But the prince is unable to learn . . . He is unkind to her . . . He betrays her trust . . . She wants to die.

Christopher (*emotionally, to himself*)   . . . What's her name?

Walley   You interested in? (*'this kind of music?'*) He's interested in (*'this kind of music'*) – Speak up!

Maud   Rusalka . . . And she returns to the limpid pool, to sink alone back into the water . . . But she knows that he, too, will never be free of her. And she waits for him to follow, to die, in understanding at last, in her arms. (*She rises.*)

Wally   Eh? . . . Sit!

She remains standing. She looks at **Christopher**.

Maud   Would you like me to leave?

Wally   What's that?

Christopher *rises. He is trembling, highly agitated, the gun pointed directly at* **Wally**.

Wally   . . . Steady on, old boy.

Christopher   I didn't find you in directories, new or old –

Wally   Please –

Christopher   You were observed walking heartily in the street!

Wally (*rising*)   Was I? Well, if you say so –

Christopher   Yesss, I say so! – No, sit!

Wally   No, please, Chris, Christopher – You in any financial bother? –

Christopher   No, no –

Wally   D'you know what I mean? – Money! – She has plenty –

Christopher   No! Sit! Sit! I never played a prank on you or called you names but I've begun to remember a matter that has started to bother me, an incident that happened in class in school one day.

Wally   Was there? Wo-ho –

Christopher   Ho!

Wally   If y'say so –

Christopher   Indeed I do say so, wo-ho-ho and ouch, elephant's brain, old boy!

Wally   Maud? (*A plea for help.*)

Maud (*quietly*)   Shoot him.

Christopher   Whilst you were standing up in class one day someone placed a drawing pin for you to sit on. Without any evidence whatsoever you decided I had put it there and then cruelly made of me another subject of your reign of terror. I told you then a hundred times and over as many days that I did not put the drawing pin there, if drawing pin there ever was that day, and I have called tonight to tell you for one last time.

Wally   T'be sure, t'be –

Christopher   No, you be sure –

Wally   If y'say so –

Christopher   No, you be sure, you say so, yes or no, to *what* I *now* *de*clare up*on* my *word* of *hon*our!

Wally   Accept!

Christopher (*sobbing*)   I'm sorry for calling so late and unannounced, Mrs Peters!

He stumbles off, gun in hand, sobbing.

The music and the figures follow him.

Scene Six

Table and the table lamp, unlit.

Christopher, *in overcoat dishevelled; a sense of futility. The earphones dangle from his hands.*

The table lamp comes on of itself. He wonders about this. A bright light falls on the table. Then another. (Lights as for television purposes.) A mike is lowered over the table. He is terrified.

Christopher   He goes to the podium with confidence. (*He stands at the table and stuffs the earphones into a pocket. Then:*) Testing: One, two, three, four, seven. (*He mouths the word, as to a television crew, off.*) More? Schopenhauer: His Phenomenology of Reproduction. (*Mouths it.*) More? And Did He Hypostatise the *Ding an sich*?

During the following, he holds a fascinated horror of himself; he has to pretend that what he's saying makes sense; and he cannot stop himself. Terror makes him smile.

He nods, having received his cue to begin. He smiles.

President. Fellow acolytes of IASA, distinguished guests, distinguished colleagues, distinguished viewers, friends, distinguished students . . . (*He gathers speed.*) The spatio-temporal world consisting of individual objects subject to the law of causality bound together by the cause-effect relation which is an a-priori form of existence though pertaining to the mind is phenomenon, is idea, but the thing-in-itself, the reality, the everything, is will, and its focus lies in the reproductive system, the ding-a-dong. (*There is something he has just said that doesn't quite make sense.*) Which gives us pought for thause . . . But! – Before! – Yes! – Because! – Before I go further – Exactly! Crass – remiss. I refer of course to my colleague and friend Dr Wuzzler who is extremely ill in . . . Actually, who passed away this morning. Alas. Speaking personally of his distinguished career and of his remarkable discovery only last year I fear no contradiction when I say I do not for a single moment believe that the young Arthur

Schopenhauer ever came next or near that little scenic port
of Cobh in Co. Cork in 1802. (*There is something there too that
he shouldn't have said.*) Another year, yes, but o two, no. And it
was certainly no mean achievement of his to hold that chair
at Trinity for twenty-eight years and a bit. But now he has a
throne. (*He acknowledges heaven.*)

Here it may be appropriate to take a look at the age
Schopenhauer was born into. The guillotine was not at all
essential. Suicide. Suicide went rampant – so unlike our own
times. Self-destruction to such an extent that records down-
through-the-ages were looked up in search of possible causes
and cures. Suicide, the incidence of *mass* suicide! Oh yes,
those have-a-happy-go-lucky-Californian-day caperers did
not create a precedent in the avocado or banana fields of –
Orange County, was it? Yes, there are seats up here at the
front, boys and girls. (*Gesturing the student section of his 'audience'
to come forward.*) Ah, the insidious appeal of suicide to the
young romantic mind!

I do not wish to overemphasise this suicide business because
I am very much against it, very much, and because – Sorry,
President? – (*He nods.*) – and because we have to push on.

So, enter Arthur Schopenhauer to take to his rooms and
have a think about it all. Did he help matters? The brevity
of life which we so lament may be it's greatest virtue, he
said. Man is a thing that ought not to be, he said. Worse, he
said: Man is a flaw containing a bigger flaw within himself,
which is the will to reproduce, blind will, the thing-in-itself,
the ding-a-dong. (*There is something again that isn't right; an aside
to himself:*) Ding-a-dong? (*No, it's fine:*) Ding-a-dong.

And *that's* why we feel guilty about doing it.

But there is a way out, because all this is very sad. And the
way out is? Knowledge. The way to stop this all-too-active,
mindless and erroneous business and get blind autonomous
willie off reproductive duty is to take matters by the head.
'For what bridle and bit are to the unmanageable horse, the

intellect is for the will of man.' In a nutshell, if only we thought about it we'd think again.

But wait a minute, knowledge is an illusion, isn't it? So where does that leave the intellect? What is he talking about? Further – exactly! The intellect comes from the mother, will from the father. He *hated* his mother. And she was a bad novelist, wasn't she? She pushed him down the stairs, didn't she? – She was a *terrible* novelist. You will say forget the staircase, what is meant is that the intellect is inherited *genetically*, from the mother: that is what I would've said too but *so-and-therefore*! the same must apply to the will coming from the father. His father was a suicide! D'you see what I mean? Died by his own hand – well, he pushed himself into the river, didn't he? – 1805, April – August then, September – probably on a Saturday. And! His paternal granny was crazy as a Danzigger coot.

Need I mention his brother? D'you see what I mean? I mean, if he says there's never to be contentment, no love lost, knowledge only an illusion, will wicked, without any ability to know, suffering the true destiny, why does *he* go on and on? For seventy-two years. Why didn't he kill himself, instead of leaving it to me? Or you. And I don't think he can have liked himself very much.

Through the above he has been searching his pockets, absently producing various items in turn and putting them on the table: a book, earphones, the gun, the cigarette, a handkerchief . . .

He must have found something to keep him going, some harmony. Sorry, President? (*He holds up the book.*) This? (*The earphones.*) These? (*The gun.*) This? (*The cigarette.*) This? (*Nods, and puts the cigarette away.*) And because we have to push on.

The bright lights, in turn, go out on him during the following and his voice, if miked, is unmiked, until he becomes a man, lost, alone in a room, talking to himself.

He lived alone, kept his distance. Loaded guns beside his bed at night. For burglars? Cheph! His career at university?

Hegel had the chair. Hegel had a suite of chairs. He had a
dog of course, called . . . forget. Atma, yes. Atma, meaning
world soul. A poodle – a toy one maybe, and not big enough
to be of threat to property, a young one and, therefore, not
having to be put down like Chokki. Chokki, meaning . . .
gentleness. What else had he? (*Cigarette is out again and he is
searching for matches.*) A pipe, yes he smoked a pipe – what
else? Tears, self-pity – yeh, they were a great help – what
else? Women. That narrow-shouldered, broad-hipped short-
legged race, he called them. Still, it didn't stop him having
his one-night stands and casual amours. But of sufficient
duration, of such effect, as to produce children. Children:
thorns of kindred. All of whom he managed to consign to
anonymity aad illegitimacy. Or did he manage that so well?
. . . And though he could not see how they could possibly
love him, could it be possible that they did? (*He can't find
matches.*) Hasn't anybody got a light? . . . Why did he take to
his rooms in the first place? He didn't care? . . . That Jack
might come home late one night mortally wounded by a
blade. That Petra, too, waylaid, innocence defiled, mouth
open, eyes dilated in the grass. Never to be found? Or that
they would take their own lives into the earth. Thorns of
kindred. *Beloved* thorns of kindred. Yes. Yes, and that she,
too, his casual amour, water-sprite and temporary wife –
Was that what she was? Patricia . . . too, would (*nods: 'die'*)
. . . or drown. And when they stopped, the kisses of that
casual amour of twenty years' duration, instead of love
letters, did he send to her for signing, affidavits, orders,
papers, to achieve that right of man to be left alone. For
what? To escape, *ease* the pain of boundless love. For what?
In order, in isolation, to achieve that other state, the terror
of memories and guilt mocking the impotence and failure of
a jumble of words.

Mind you, he did, genuinely, like animals. Could that have
kept him going? The aforementioned little anal poodle thing
– Atma. And he wrote something about porcupines, didn't
he? What was it? Porcupines – hedgehogs – What was it?
Tck! (*He can't remember.*)

What is the resolution, boys and girls? (*Sighs.*) Does it have to be suicide? Reconciliation: too late? Blasted hedgehogs? . . . Bury Cornelia first.

Music up, figures gathering, babble of voices.

Scene Seven

*A post-funeral feast at **Michael**'s place. **Michael** looks well and he is impeccably dressed. **Patricia** is present, happy and relaxed. **Petra** in a long Arab-type wedding dress (the square of bodice done in coloured threads and beads). An issue isn't made of it but she is unforgiving of **Tony**: she ignores him. **Jack** is enthusiastic, it's like Christmas to him; he has drink and a cigar. **Geoffrey** and **Tony** are on their best behaviour; **Tony**, as before, is cued into action by **Geoffrey**. **Monica** has a new hairdo – or maybe it's a hat. And there is **Moreva**, a new girlfriend of **Jack**'s, who wears jeans with a man's check shirt hanging outside them; almost throughout, she reads a thick paperback.*

*They are drinking wine and there's beer for later for those who want it. And **Michael** is going to open a bottle of champagne.*

Christopher, *in his overcoat, at a remove from them, watches for a while before joining the scene.*

Jack   That was *lovely* lamb.

Monica   Did you like it, Jack?

Jack   Oh God, it was lovely!

Monica   Did you have enough, Geoffrey?

Geoffrey   First rate, a sufficiency! Tony!

Tony   Top class!

Geoffrey   Thank you!

Tony   Thank you very much! Full marks!

Michael   Well, you can thank Monica! (*He is undoing the champagne.*)

Monica   Good heavens – heavens – he cooked it himself!

Patricia   Oh! Michael, I'd forgotten. (*A bottle of champagne from her feet in a paper bag.*)

Michael   You shouldn't have, Patricia! (*See:*) I'd got some in.

Monica   He's a wonderful cook.

Michael   Are you all right, love?

Patricia   Yes!

Michael   Should I call over one evening?

Patricia   No!

Tony   That's a very peculiar dress – Petra. (*He means 'lovely'.*)

Petra   Uncle Michael, is there a pint glass in the house?

Michael   Everybody! Wait for it . . . (*Champagne cork pops.*)

Jack   An angel's fart!

Michael *starts to circle the table, pouring the champagne.* **Monica** *and* **Patricia** *start to clear things away.*

Monica   Let us make a little space for you.

Patricia   No, you sit down, Monica –

Monica   I'll do no such thing, Patricia! –

Patricia   You've been on your feet all morning!

Geoffrey   Tony! ('*Help with the clearing away.*')

Monica   Shall we leave it to Tony then? (*The women laugh as they clear up.*)

Jack   The champagne is going to take all day – Petra, pass us down that bottle there!

Patricia   Easy does it now, m'boy!

Petra (*to* **Jack**)   D'you want beer?

Patricia   And m'girl! You didn't do very well with your plate, Monica.

Monica   Tummy. (*A lie.*) Have the men all had enough now?

Tony (*clearing* **Petra**'s *plate*)   Allow me – Petra. You have a very peculiar name.

Petra   Uncle Michael, can we open the beer?

Michael   Good grief!

Christopher *has joined them.*

Monica   Christopher, my dear!

Patricia   Christopher!

Monica   My dear, my *dear*!

Patricia   Come in, come in, so pleased you could make it!

Monica   Always lovely to see you!

Patricia   Where shall we put you?

Petra   Pint bloody glass anywhere?

Michael (*sighing;* **Christopher**'s *arrival is most inconvenient to his management.*)   Have you eaten, because as you can see we are clearing things away?

Christopher   I have.

Michael   Pardon?

Monica   Are you sure?

Christopher   I've eaten.

Patricia   Where would you like to sit?

Michael   Anywhere! (*And he continues his round with the champagne.*)

Christopher   I've eaten.

Monica   I understand.

Michael   Everybody! *Please* hold your champagne for the toast, there's plenty of it but don't-drink-it-yet!

Monica and **Patricia**, *chatting, go off (to the kitchen) with lunch things.*

Jack (*self-consciously*)   Hi.

Christopher (*self-conscious of* **Jack**, *nodding, smiling*) How're you?

Jack (*nodding*)   Would you like a glass of wine?

Christopher   Yeh.

Geoffrey   The hard man! (*Shakes hands with* **Christopher**.) A bit of high spirits the other evening. (*Calls:*) Tony son, don't you have something for someone?

Tony   Geoffrey! (*He has a present for* **Christopher** *and as he goes out to fetch it:*) Privilege to be here!

Geoffrey   He's my nephew, we're in business together. He's a university man too, you know? Oh yes, he was a student for years and years.

Jack   Dad? (*A glass of wine to* **Christopher**.)

Geoffrey   Studied to be an architect, but he never practised, so we're in animal feed together.

Jack   Dad? (*He has pulled up a chair for* **Christopher**.)

Michael   Now, would everyone mind sitting down again, please!

Geoffrey   So, when we came down here on Wednesday and swung a big one: bit of high spirits.

Jack   Good luck?

Christopher   Cheers! (*They clink glasses.*)

Michael   Is she all right, Jack? – Are you all right, love?

Moreva *looks up, smiles-nods, and returns to her book.*

Jack   Did you smoke?

Christopher   No. (**Jack** *smiles, dubious.*) I didn't.

Jack   Would you like a cigar? (*He laughs.*)

Michael   Everybody, please! (*'Be seated.'*) Patricia, Monica! Where's Tony?

Geoffrey   Tony!

Tony (*returning*)   You supply the birds, we'll provide the cages! (*He has a small box.*)

Geoffrey   D'you get it? He studied architecture –

Petra (*calling*)   Mum, Monica, speech! –

Geoffrey   Y'don't get it? – It's an architect's joke!

Christopher   Mmmah!

Michael   Christopher, *please*! Geoffrey, Jack.

Geoffrey   OK, Mike. (*And a finger to his lips to* **Tony**, *to leave the presentation of the box until later.*)

Monica *and* **Patricia** *are returning to their seats.*

Monica   No, the lamb was Michael's idea. I hope I'm not speaking out of turn, Patricia, but turkey, poultry for a funeral; meat, flesh: no. Or is that just me?

And they laugh and sit.

Michael   Now, has everyone got a glass of –

Jack   Silence! Michael is going to make a speech!

Michael   Champagne, everybody?

Geoffrey   OK, Mike.

Michael   Ladies and –

Jack   Silence, everybody!

Patricia   Jack.

Tony   OK, Mike.

Michael   The service was short. That is how Cornelia would have liked it. This feast which we have just had is how she would have liked it: family, friends, acquaintances around her own table. Thank you all again for coming. The reason why the Reverend Lavelle isn't here to say a few words which I asked him to prepare is because he had to go off and bury somebody else.

Jack   Pass down that bottle again.

Michael   I have no way of knowing what those words would have been –

Jack   D'you want some?

Tony   No thank you –

Michael   But I should like to say –

Tony   Jack.

Michael   But I should like to say, everybody, that Cornelia's death was not in vain. I am not a churchgoer myself, but I believe in immortality. Whatever others might believe in. My brother, for instance. Death, everybody, is not the end. Is *not* the end. Nor is it a disintegration. Death opens unknown doors. It is most grand to die.

Christopher   John Masefield.

Michael   . . . John Masefield. How wonderful is death. Death and its brother, death and its brother –

Christopher   Sleep.

Michael   Sleep.

Christopher   Shelley.

Michael (*nods, grudgingly*)   Shelley. And how wonderful –
how wonderful Cornelia feels now, seeing her sleep bringing
families and friends and acquaintances together – bringing
families together who-God-knows should be together! That
her sleep can transform *acquaintances* into lasting, lifelong
friends. Witness: Tony, Geoffrey and – sorry, Jack's
girlfriend, name please?

Jack   What's your name?

Moreva   Moreva.

Michael   Pardon?

Jack   Moreva.

Michael   And Moreva from Frankfurt.

Jack   No!

Michael   Pardon?

Jack   She's gone back.

Michael   Pardon?

Jack   That was someone else.

Michael   I see.

Petra   Would you like a cigarette, Mum? (*She's making a
rollie.*)

Patricia   Thank you, love, thank you.

Michael   Speaking of friendship, I should like to make an
especial word of thanks to Monica for –

Monica   He cooked it himself! – Good heavens! – He's a
wonderful, wonderful, wonderful cook! He's –

Michael   Monica – Monica! Monica kindly offered her
place, the Abbey, for this – celebration.

Monica   Oh! I understand.

Michael   But this is how Cornelia would have liked it.

Geoffrey   Around her own table, Mike.

Michael *nods solemnly.*

Tony   And his – Geoffrey.

Petra   Mum? (*Cigarette to* **Patricia**.)

Monica   But wasn't it a long hold-over, Michael?

Michael   Pardon?

Monica   Big Dennis himself commented. Cornelia's waiting all that time to be interred.

Michael   Her generosity, love. (*Such a well-told lie that he believes it himself.*)

Monica   Michael?

Geoffrey   Son?

Petra   Shit! (*Her lighter doesn't work.*)

Michael   She donated everything.

Geoffrey   Parts.

Michael   Though she was ill –

Petra   The fucking thing was new.

Patricia   Love.

Tony (*fervently*)   I wish I'd known her.

Michael   Though she was ill, everybody –

Geoffrey   Her words, Mike, were?

Petra   Give a poxy light to Mum, Jack.

Michael   Her words were: Take any part of me that's good that will benefit mankind.

Jack   Mum? (*And gives her a light.*)

Geoffrey   And that's generosity.

Tony   Generosity.

Michael   And that takes time.

Patricia   That colour suits you, Jack.

Monica   Any part, any organ: that would be Cornelia.

Michael   Signed on the dotted line.

Patricia (*to* **Jack**)   Very, very nice.

Petra   She loved parties, didn't she? – Jack, give us your matches here! –

Michael   Further –

Petra   Shouldn't we have some music?

Michael   Further –

Monica   She *adored* parties! Oh the things Cornelia got up to! My *dear*! You don't have to tell me, Petra! If only we could sit down and write a book, Patricia!

Monica, **Petra** *and* **Patricia** *laughing*.

Michael   A moment please! Further, everybody, Cornelia's dying this very week cannot be written away to coincidence. She could have died any week she liked. But her dying this week, I cannot help believing, was another mark of her generosity. And thoughtfulness. She was very well aware that I had taken a year off work: that year ends tomorrow, Saturday, and I must, I simply must return to work on Monday.

Petra   Uncle Michael –

Jack   The toast! – (*'For God's sake get on with it!'*)

Petra   Uncle Michael –

Geoffrey   To Cornelia! –

Tony   To –

Michael   Geoffrey, Jack, Tony! – What, love?

Petra   Wasn't there a guitar in the house?

Michael   Banjo, love? Bedroom somewhere? (*Vaguely; though he indicates the direction of the bedroom.*)

Jack   'The man he comes to see me, says the trees shimmer red –'

Michael   A moment please, Jack –

Petra   Would that be in order, Mum?

Patricia   Quite in order.

Michael   Very much in order, but – Petra! (**Petra** *has gone to the bedroom.*) She left a final message: I want everyone to hear.

He has produced a slip of paper, Cornelia's final message. It induces a silence. **Patricia** *smokes her cigarette. When they speak, they talk in whispers while awaiting* **Petra**'s *return.*

Jack   . . . (*sotto voce*) 'And outside the night deepens . . .' (*He continues to mouth the words of his song.*)

Monica   . . . Did you design that yourself, Patricia?

Patricia (*nods that she designed her own dress. Then, smiles 'are you'*)   All right, Christopher?

He nods, smiles that he is.

Monica   And you're opening a business.

Patricia   Next week. I found a premises.

Monica   You're so clever.

Geoffrey   . . . Tony. (*Cueing* **Tony** *to make his presentation.*)

Tony *tiptoes to* **Christopher** *to present him with the box.*

Tony (*whispering*)   It'll record at fifty paces. Ultra-sleek model.

Christopher   Thank you.

Geoffrey   It's got – (*He demonstrates that it's got earphones.*)

Tony   Batteries. (*Separately.*) And if you ever need a load of bran nuggets. Any quantity. (*He tiptoes back to his place.*)

Jack   . . . 'The man he comes to see me.'

Patricia (*calls*)   Petra, come at once, Michael is waiting!

Petra (*off*)   Found it! Coming!

Michael   Is she all right, Jack? Are you all right, love?

Moreva *smiles and puts down her book.*

Petra (*returns, blowing dust off a guitar / banjo / bouzouki*)   I think the strings are bolixed.

Jack   Show it here.

Patricia   Just a little longer now, children.

Michael   A last message from Cornelia. (*He reads.*) 'Death is . . . Death is . . .' (*He has become emotional, contains it suitably, and:*) Perhaps it would be more fitting coming from her sister. Would you mind very much, love?

Patricia (*reads*)   'Death is nothing at all. I have only slipped away into the next room. I am I, you are you, whatever we were to each other we are still. Call me by my own familiar name, speak to me in the easy way we always used. Put no sadness into your tone, wear no air of sorrow, laugh as we always laughed at the little jokes together. Play, smile, think of me. Life means all that it ever meant, it is the same that it ever was. There is absolute unbroken continuity. What is this death but a negligible accident? Why should I be out of mind because I am out of sight? I am but waiting for you for an interval, somewhere very near, just around the corner. All is well.'

Tears, embraces, handshakes, kisses.

Monica (*dabbing her eyes*)   Oh my dear, oh my dears I am so happy.

Petra   Mum, I love you.

Patricia   I know, love.

Petra *kisses* **Michael**. **Patricia** *holds up her hand in a gentle wave to* **Christopher**. *He smiles, bows.*

Tony   Jack? (*A handshake.*)

Jack   Would you like a cigar?

Tony   Never use them, I don't have television and I'm about to take up hang-gliding.

Monica   Such wonderful, wonderful sentiments, what can one say?

Patricia *hands the slip of paper back to* **Michael**. **Michael** *holds it up before pocketing it and, then, to* **Christopher**.

Michael   So, you see!

Christopher   Cornelia? (*'Cornelia wrote that?'*)

Michael (*nods solemnly, as is his wont; then*)   *In*-correct! Canon Henry Scott Holland, 1847–1919. So, you don't know everything. (*And, now, he laughs.*) Drink up, everybody! – Open house! – Drink up! What's your name again, love? (*And he starts to chat up* **Moreva**.)

Patricia   Michael! The toast!

Michael   To Canon Henry Scott Holland!

Patricia   To Cornelia, to my sister!

Others   To Cornelia!

Patricia   And to everyone here present.

They drink. There's laughter. **Jack** (*mends/has mended the 'bolixed' strings*) *tunes and strums the guitar.* **Petra** *has a pint glass and fills it with beer.*

Michael   To love, Moreva! Good grief, she is reading *War and Peace*! Good grief, she has nearly finished it!

Jack (*plays and sings*)   'The man he comes to see me / Says the trees shimmer red / And reflect big yellow leaves in light / That laugh at us in fadin' beauty.'

Petra   Jack, d'you mind!

Jack   'So yeh go for a swim in the limpid pool / And there you see mermaids –'

Petra   It was my idea! (*She wants to sing.*)

Jack   Push off! 'Slivers of blue translucent fins / Turn to the crimson sun.' (*Strums / finer tuning.*)

Christopher (*has moved to* **Petra**)   How many of those can you drink? (*Pints.*)

Petra   Nine. Ten. (*Defiant glance:*) Eleven?

He nods, as if impressed. He has a flower in his hand, a red rose, but he is unsure of how to present it. And, though it would appear to be for her, she cannot be sure of it.

It just goes through you.

He nods. He puts the flower down somewhere nearby and moves on.

Jack   'Struttin' girls with tinsel hair / lavish misery on screamin' hounds / Tear from the moon a silver shroud / A misty veil of sick-stained air.'

Christopher   Not bad.

Jack   Author?

Christopher   Askey?

Jack (*laughs*)   'Your mind rips through the tangled room / Bodies emanatin' filthy smoke / Twistin' carcasses writhin' wet / Your head explodes, you can't forget.' (*And strums a little.*) 'So yeh pick up your clothes, walk out the door / Your feet leave impressions on red bits of floor.' (*Strums.*)

Christopher   Good stuff. I'd watch my back over there if I were you: your uncle Michael would tip a cat going out a skylight.

Jack, *still strumming, laughs, then shrugs 'Moreva is just a friend'.*

Christopher   But are my quotations improving? (*He is moving on again.*)

Jack   Dad? . . . I'm sorry about the other night.

Christopher   No, I'm sorry, Jack.

Jack   I'm the one who has to prove something.

Christopher   I think you're getting there. (*He moves on.*)

Jack (*is pleased*)   'And outside the night deepens, darkness descends / The man says your head is right / The man says your head's now right, the nightmare begins!' (*Which is a bit of a triumph for* **Jack**.)

And, indeed, somewhere around here, **Michael**, *with* **Moreva** *in tow and a bottle of champagne, slips off to the bedroom.*

Geoffrey *and* **Tony** *are putting on their coats.*

Geoffrey   Well, God bless all! God bless! Tony.

Tony   Privilege!

Geoffrey   God bless!

Tony   Privilege.

Goodbyes. They leave. **Monica** *and* **Patricia** *have done more clearing away.* **Monica**, *too, is putting on her coat.*

Monica   Well, do you know, Patricia, honestly and truly, people are wonderful, they're so nice. And do you know it *is* all about love. Honestly, I'm still crying inside.

Patricia   Jack, give Petra a hand to replace those tables to where they belong.

Monica   And I'll see you soon again, please God. (*Fingering* **Patricia**'s *dress:*) So, so clever. Jack, Petra: Sweetheart. Sweetheart. (*She kisses them.*) I must be getting home to my treasure. He's holding the fort, he can be very good at times, the chiefest among ten thousand.

Patricia   'I sat down in his shadow with great delight'!

Monica   I sat down in his shadow – Isn't it wonderful? – The Song of Solomon!

And the two women celebrate it with a laugh, together.

And my dear Christopher! (*Kisses him. Then:*) But *you* should be able to write a book – or a play? Have you ever tried? (*And she tweaks his cheek:*) Oh, if we could only simply keep you as pets! (*And she's gone.*)

Christopher *and* **Patricia**, *together, now find they are shy of each other.*

Christopher   How are you? (*She smiles.*) . . . Hmm?

Patricia   No, how are *you*, which is more important.

Christopher   No, how are *you*? Which is more important.

Patricia   I'm fine.

Christopher   You've lost weight.

Patricia   I've gained! Women put it on when things go . . . (*'wrong'*); men lose it. And Michael is like a skeleton. Where is he?

Christopher   I think I saw him go into the – out for a breath of fresh air.

Patricia   We have to be going in a minute.

'Yes,' he nods. They'll be going their separate ways in a moment.

. . . Like a nightmare, wasn't it? The past six months.

He nods.

. . . How did we arrive at this point in time?

He nods.

. . . But I'm fine now. And you?

Christopher   Yeh!

Patricia   Are you looking after yourself?

Christopher   Yeh!

Patricia   Oh! And Petra was saying you're working on something very important.

Christopher   Mmm!

Patricia   Yes?

Christopher   No, you were saying earlier – I overheard you saying you've got a shop?

Patricia (*'yes'*)   I'm looking forward to it. And I wanted to apologise.

Christopher   For what?

Patricia   Oh . . . (*'lots of things'*). And those papers from the solicitor that I've been neglecting to sign.

Christopher   I haven't been pushing them. I haven't! I mean, that was – that was the solicitor. (*He has an inclination to laugh.*) I mean, there's no hurry . . . Is there?

Patricia   I was in his office yesterday and I took the opportunity. And I find I'm at peace now. We have cried enough. You've been extraordinarily kind to me. Thank you.

Petra *and* **Jack** – *singing, laughing, perhaps, swapping snatches of* **Jack**'s *song* – *have been 'replacing' the furniture, until there is only a single table and table lamp, phone and answering machine left.*

Patricia   Well done, children! Now get your coats. (*To* **Christopher**:) But they're great, aren't they?

Christopher   I didn't know how great.

Patricia   Wherever we got them from.

Christopher   Blind will.

Patricia (*laughs 'What?'*)   Well, take care now, won't you? All the best.

Christopher   Bye.

Jack *waves to him from the door.* **Petra**, **Patricia** *and* **Jack** *leave.*

Lights changing. **Christopher**, *alone, isolated, feels his pockets. He finds the gun and the cigarette. He has a choice to make. But he has no light.*

Christopher (*whispers*)   Help . . . Help.

Petra *returns, ostensibly to collect her hat. (He holds the gun behind his back.)*

Petra   My bloodywell hat. Oh, I thought everyone had gone. (*Then, the flower:*) Is this for me? (*He nods.*) An olive branch?

Christopher   No, it's a rose.

She takes the rose, smiles to herself, dumps a box of matches (**Jack**'s) *on the table and leaves, putting on her hat.*

Nothing is what's happened here.

He lights the cigarette and draws deeply on it.

Instead, after long and penitential abstinence, he rejoined the persecuted minority of smokers in slow death. Draft two. President, fellow acolytes of IASA, ladies and –

The phone is ringing. He lifts it and replaces it on the cradle.

But, here, before giving my paper, it might be appropriate to take a preamble from the *Paralipomena*. A group of porcupines – hedgehogs – on a winter's day crowded close together to save themselves from the cold by their mutual warmth. Soon, however, they felt each other's spines and this drove them apart again. Whenever their need brought them back together, this discomfort intervened until, thrown this way and that between the cold and the spines, they found a moderate distance from one another at which they could survive best.

*The figures have returned, music comes up, the figures are circling him.
He looks at the gun.*

It probably didn't work anyway.

*As the figures close on him, he appears to be tossing the gun away and
there is a bang.*